How Not to Blog:
Finding Myself, One Post
at A Time

Kali Desautels

For Shaeli and Liam
Mama Loves You

Hey everybody,

You know that dream that you hold in your heart forever, and are kind of afraid that it won't ever come true? Well, you are holding mine. I have wanted to" be *a writer"* since I was a little girl and learned that these magical things were written by real humans. My childhood heroines were all writers – Jo March from *Little Women*, Anne Shirley from *Anne of Green Gables*, Laura Ingalls from the *Little House* books. As I grew older, my inspiration continued to be found in works by women who wrote everything down, and sent it out into the world, hoping for an audience. Joan Didion, Maeve Brennan, Toni Morrison, Hope Jahren, Rachel Hollis, Maya Angelou, Brené Brown, Gloria Steinem, Caitlin Moran, Zadie Smith, Chimamanda Ngozi Adichie, Lindy West... I could write an entire book that is essential a list of amazing women who write amazing books.

How Not to Blog is exactly that – what you should not do if you are wanting to build a following. My posts are any length that I decide to make them. They take you through obsessive loves for things like *Doctor Who, Supernatural,* and *Sherlock*; my work in advocating for mental health; career changes; my marriage; my freaking amazing kids; my cranky cat; my incredible friends; my beautiful, funny, wildly unique family; and most of all, they are just me. My thoughts in the world.

So, if you are reading this book because you are looking for a great guide for how to start a blog, I am sorry to say that this is not it. But if you are looking for a friend who loves you and is honest, even when it's hard, come on in. I think we will get along just fine!

Love,
Kali
P.S. it's pronounced Kaylee, not Callie. I swear.

WRITING

February 20, 2017

Having been a book lover and reader all my life, I had a fantasy of one day writing my own book. The idea of completing an original idea, setting it to paper, and, ambitiously, seeing it printed in hard copy with my name emblazoned on the front cover has always been a secret wish of mine. But lack of confidence, fear of failure and the constraints that are Life stepped in my way and kept me from allowing this to be anything more than a wish. Then, suddenly, as if by some chance rather than by design, I decided to write.  And write. And write. The more I read of other writers' works, the more I felt inspired to write. I began with the hope that I would complete a NaNoWriMo (National Novel Writing Month) novel, but it became clear that I could not produce the book of my wish, the book I would be proud of, nor the book that would allow me to neither neglect my children, nor my day job, in one month. So, I began to plan. I could see the characters that I wanted to create, and I knew the world they would populate, but I needed to create their story. Now, three months into the writing process, I have completed more than 20% of my first draft (with a 90,000-word goal) and hope to have the first draft completed by Fall.

Please bear with me as I make sidebar use of my blog to discuss the trials and tribulations of sticking with it, and turning a wish into a goal, and hopefully, one day, a realization.

HAPPINESS

February 21, 2017

My laptop and I have been fast friends for the last few months. I had neglected her a while, but since this writing wish has turned into a writing goal, the big, cumbersome, slow old gal and I are on good terms. I appreciate that she ain't

what she used to be, but I know exactly where all the keys are. (*Not all keyboards are created equal.*) She is slow, but when the screen lights up, and I click on my Word icon, I feel happy. I feel pride and I feel like this is what I absolutely want to be doing. The words don't always flow and I have not mastered the art of silencing my inner editor, but sitting on my reading chair, a blanket across my lap, earbuds playing variations of classical music on SoundCloud, with my cat at my side, my kitchen timer under him (*seriously… he will not **not** lay on it*), I feel like I am working on something for me, and I am happy. Maybe it will become a real, honest to goodness, published piece of literature, or maybe it will simply be 90,000 words of my soul typed into a very old laptop, making my heart happy. Either way, my laptop and I will keep up our sometimes frustrating, but always rewarding friendship.

THE DARING OF PEGGY FLASH FICTION

February 21, 2017

Dear Reader,

The following post is an excerpt from the novel that I have been writing for the past 3 years and is not yet finished. One day…

Please indulge me.

Love Kali

Peggy sat down. She chose the bench farthest away from the crowd. It was out of the sun, and in late November, on the rare warm, late autumn day, retreating from the sun is not a common choice. Peggy was not a common girl. Or rather, I suppose, she was not a common woman. The office buildings seemed to have emptied themselves of their human contents, spilling them into the sun, as they sought their short spell of rest; their respite from the usual daily drudgery.
From her vantage point, set back and away from most other people, Peggy could see where the trees and the sky reversed themselves into the ocean. With not even a breeze in the warm air, the ocean was a mirror: the dark green trees rising up at the waters' edge, also pointed themselves downward, into and through the ocean, as though trying to escape the confines of the upward expectation that people generally held for trees.
Peggy smoothed out her thick, brown, woollen skirt and crossed her ankles. Satisfied that passersby would be duly impressed by the picture she created of herself, as they walked on, enjoying their surprise constitutional for the day. Peggy was unaware of how little attention the passersby afforded her. In fact, although she intended to appear shy or retiring by selecting a lonesome bench, in truth, Peggy was not the least bit shy. In her mind, she could clearly see that all who passed her way were glancing in her direction, undoubtedly admiring her as a sweet portrait of young womanhood – the full skirt, the well-tailored red jacket, the neat, though slightly scuffed pumps, the bangs on her heart-shaped face swept neatly to one side. Her green eyes were bright, though slightly small for her face. She felt that this flaw was offset by the perfect Cupid's Bow of her small mouth. Her nose was spiced with a dash of freckles and upturned into a darling button. She was a proud woman, proud of her appearance, proud of her cleverness.

On this day, as she settled herself to enjoy her small paper cup filled with hot coffee, Peggy felt particularly clever. Working as a typist at a large newspaper, Peggy had achieved a modest level of success. After all, she was a woman. This was an ideal career. A holding pattern, until a suitable man came to sweep her off to the suburbs. She had dared to picture herself as a journalist. This ambition wasn't unheard of, there was a smattering of lady writers at the paper, and Peggy was assuredly much more eloquent and intelligent than they. The only stumbling block seemed to be that the journalists and editors did not take her seriously enough and told her that she must earn her position; that patience was a virtue. Well, bully for virtue, she smirked. Her patience had worn through, and she had done something so daring, she hardly would have believed it, had she not done it herself. Whilst typing Mr. Brennan's wretched piece, it struck her that the man had hardly the wits that God gave a cat, and methodically began to unspool the paper from the typewriter. With a slow smile, Peggy recalled how she had crumpled the ludicrous article and gently dropped it from her elegant tapered fingers into the wire waste paper basket at her feet. Quickly, and perhaps a tad furtively, she loaded a fresh sheet into the machine and set to typing. Her tongue passed over her lips in concentration as she prepared her story. The clacking of her keys had never sounded so cheerful to her ears as they did at that moment. When finished, she quickly scrawled Mr. Brennan's name on an envelope and neatly folded her story.

Peggy was certain that when Mr. Brennan read her story, he would undoubtedly prefer it to his own senseless drivel. She felt light on her toes as she placed it on his desk, before leaving the office to sit, as we find her, on the dimly lit bench, intent on drawing attention to herself, by appearing to not draw attention to herself. Sipping her coffee, Peggy felt the warmth of the day, and the warmth of her dark, decadent beverage, and the warmth of her daring.

It was only a matter of time before she settled herself in the soon to be the former office of that talentless Mr. Brennan.

Or perhaps jobless, back in her rooms at the boarding house…

PINK SHIRT DAY 2017

February 22, 2017

Today, it is not about writing. It is not about great and not so great books. It is about Amanda Todd, Rehteah Parsons, Sladjana Vidovic, Phoebe Prince, Tyler Clementi, Jamie Hubley, Audrie Pott, Kenneth Wisehuhn, Jadin Bell, Emilie Olsen, Nakia Venant, and the thousands of other kids and teens who were bullied to death. Today is not about generalized schoolyard teasing, it is not about friends ribbing each other good-humoredly. Today is about a culture of sustained, aggravated, malicious, intensive maltreatment of fellow human beings, to the point that no intervention will do anything to stop it. To the point that the victim sees no alternative other than to end it all. Today is Anti-Bullying Day.
Across the world today, we are wearing pink shirts, and it is not because "On Wednesdays, we wear pink". It is because kids, such as those portrayed in Tina Fey's *Mean Girls* (from whence we learned the above quote), have taken meanness too far. It is because adults have been conditioned to look out "for number one", and that "it's not personal, it's just business", to the point that there is an environment of high school bullying in the workplace. I have heard over the years that everyone is bullied and that we need to have thicker skin, but that has little of anything to do with actual bullying. I was teased for being a goody-goody, a teacher's pet, and a crybaby. It hurt, and I didn't like it, but that wasn't bullying. That is kids being mean. When kids from hate groups that are designed to do nothing but pick on one girl, until she must change schools to rediscover herself worth, *that* is bullying. When the internet allows for gossip to spread quicker than a California brush fire, when images can be photoshopped and texted to an entire class, when school halls spread into the world, and the girl who changes schools finds that her new school has already been poisoned against her before she even stepped foot in the door – that is bullying in today's world. We used to be able to leave the teasing at school, and if it went on, we would pretend to have the flu for a day or two, but eventually, that sort of meanness would move along to the next weakest person. Now the school halls are everywhere. They are in bed where the victim seeks refuge with his cellphone to escape the misery. They are in the movie theatre, where the victim's phone buzzes with each vitriolic tweet. They are everywhere. Today, we remind each

other that this must stop. Today, we show the victims that we are listening to them.

That said, we *must* truly listen. We cannot simply don a pink shirt, feel benevolent and move on. Today is not about just today. Tomorrow, when we all change back into our black shirts, we need to remain allies. We need to speak to our kids about what is acceptable behaviour. We need to remember that teens think adults are out of touch and create interventions that will allow them to feel loved and supported. We need to teach children that there is no excuse for this.

And we need to define the difference between kids being mean, and bullying. I have noticed that "bullying" has become shorthand for "he won't play with me", and "she made fun of my drawing", and I feel that the watering down of the word is doing bullying victims a serious disservice. What happens when we hear the same word over and over? We become desensitized to it, and instead of taking bullying allegations seriously, we instruct our children to learn to deal with it. But that is not possible. How do you just "deal" with the I Hate Hannah Club? How do you just "deal" with photos of your rape being used as "evidence" of your promiscuity? How do you just "deal" with a grown man in a completely different country cyberstalking you, a child, and ensuring that no matter where you go, you will be tormented? The answer is that you can't. You need help.

This morning, my son, who has worn his pink shirt any day of the year, cried when we reminded him to wear it. He had been teased and told that "pink is a girl's colour" (which opens a whole other can of worms about gender discrimination. But that is for another post on another day.), and due to that teasing, he did not want to wear pink. When we got to daycare, there was the boy that had teased him, wearing a pink shirt. The point is that, yes, kids can be mean. They can lash out and say mean things without thinking. It can make you cry, but we need Pink Shirt Day for this reason – if the meanness is allowed to continue, it can grow; we need to learn ourselves, and teach our children that under no circumstances is it ok to intentionally hurt another person. Ever. There is a large percentage of the global population that believes that bullying is the best way to get ahead, and sadly, we reinforce this by promoting bullies, by electing them to the highest offices, by deferring to them. But today is about making this stop. Today is about remembering those who didn't survive their bullying, speaking up for those who are being bullied now, and for beginning the discussion that will allow us to move forward, into a kinder society.

I PRONOUNCE IT "KAYLEE"

February 24, 2017

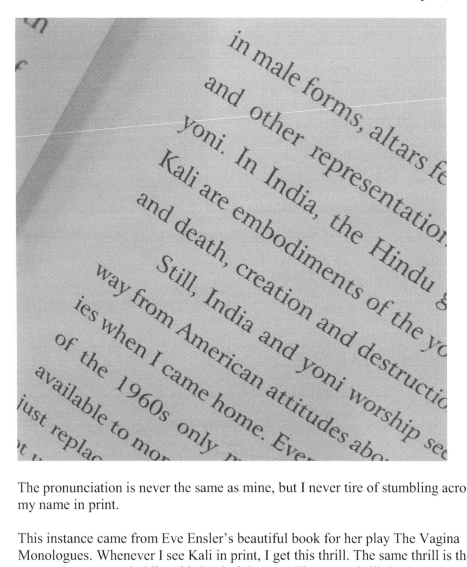

The pronunciation is never the same as mine, but I never tire of stumbling across my name in print.

This instance came from Eve Ensler's beautiful book for her play The Vagina Monologues. Whenever I see Kali in print, I get this thrill. The same thrill is the reason that you are holding this book right now. The same thrill that causes me to sit down at my laptop and string words together until they become a sentence, and then the sentences together until they become a paragraph, then an essay, and then finally something that someone, somewhere can read. Something that might cause someone to think about a perspective they may have been unaware of before.

There is something so magical about a book that when you find your name in it, you feel like maybe the magic is touching you, too. When I was in university, I took an entire course on Eastern Religions, because there was a component on my namesake Goddess Kali (Kah-li, though). I wanted to learn more about the Goddess to whom so many attribute my name. The reason that after nearly 40 years I still get asked "how does it feel to be named after the Hindu goddess of Death and Destruction?" Well, sister, let me tell you – that is a pretty vague interpretation of Kali-ma. The woman was more than death and destruction, the woman is about burning it all down, and raising back up. She embodies the feminine energy or *shakti*. She is the goddess of death, violence, and destruction, sure, but she is also the symbol for mother love. So, if I *had* been named after Kali, I would have to say that I feel great about it.

But no, my name is not Kali as in Kah-li. My name is Kali as in the Polynesian translation of my mother's name, changed ever so slightly so that I would not spend my life pronouncing it to people. And yet here I am – the opening chapter to my first book, explaining how to pronounce my name, and why it is what it is. My mom travelled to Hawaii as a teenager and saw that many of the letters in her name were not included in the Hawaiian alphabet – most particularly the pair of "R"s in the middle. Instead, she found her name translated to Keli, as in Hawaiian, the letter "E" is pronounced like a hard "A" in English. So, Keli was pronounced like Kaylee. She decided that this was a beautiful name and that she did not want people to mispronounce my name as the more common and more popular Kelly. Thus, the "E" was replaced with an "A" and Keli became Kali. I have been asked for years why this is my name, I was told by a substitute teacher that the way I pronounce my name is disrespectful, I have gotten used to looking up when I hear "Callie Dezzzz…oh… Dez-ought-uhls?" called in a doctor's waiting room. I have found a cadre of friends who have varying levels of difficulty to their names, whether it be spelling, pronunciation, first or last. I come from an entire generation of people who were named in defiance of the Susans and Donnas and Christophers of the previous generation. So, instead of seeing and hearing my name everywhere, like my conventionally named husband, Dave, seeing Kali in print, on paper, in a book provides that frisson of recognition. The magic reaching out of the book and bringing me in. Including me in the story.

ON A PERSONAL NOTE

March 26, 2017

It doesn't take much.

A week ago, I was in Hawaii with my best friend, enjoying the sun, the beach and each other's company. The flight home was a red-eye, and I did not think to set an alarm or prepare in any way for the fact that my medications, taken diligently every single night at bedtime, would be required, regardless that I would not be sleeping. I carry my medication with me on all planes, in case of an emergency or a lost suitcase, but I did not think of the feeling of emergency that would be 48 hours without my fibromyalgia, Hashimoto's, migraine and anxiety medications.

After my 24-hour trip home, meds safely in my carry on, I proceeded to collapse into a bed of exhaustion, thereby missing my second doses of medication. The next morning, I rose early, to get to work after a week away, without a thought to the medications, as morning is not medication time in my world. I was happy to be at work and functioning at a normal level when I became mildly dizzy. Deciding it must be hunger, and jet lag, I took a late lunch break. This did nothing to assuage my dizziness and light-headedness. I am sure I am not the only chronic illness sufferer who begins to feel a wave of panic when their bodies suddenly take over their brains. After work, I walked to the train, realizing that I was having trouble finding my footing. Vertigo and anxiety do not make good bedfellows and I felt nausea and fear take over. I sat through the train ride, willing myself to function, willing my vision to clear and my mind to resume normal capacity, when it occurred to me that I had gone cold turkey, unwittingly, for 52 hours, off Cymbalta, Amitriptyline, Synthroid, and my various supplements, none of which is safe. Every medication I consume requires doctor-supervised weaning, not an immediate stoppage. I was entering withdrawal from medications I had no desire to stop taking. By the time the train arrived at my stop an hour later, I was confused, disoriented, nauseated, panicked and absolutely in no condition to drive. I called my husband, who came to take me home and immediately took all the chemicals and synthetic hormones that my body needs to function at a level even remotely like where a healthy person is naturally. After a few hours, my brain began to de-fog, my head steadied, my panic subsided. I felt better.

But it doesn't take much.

A few days later, I feel my depression like a worn housecoat; I feel the pain in my joints; I feel the fatigue which gnaws at me; I see a blur in my vision. I am better, but not. I am back to the beginning and know it will be days, if not weeks before I regain the sense of calm and health that have taken years and medications to achieve. And I cannot be angry with my flawed body, as I had the keys to avoid this in my bag. I took for granted the feeling of wellness provided by my pharmaceuticals and my learned doctors and pushed myself into a setback.

And clearly, it doesn't take much.

PINTEREST-ING OURSELVES INTO HUXLEY'S BRAVE NEW WORLD

March 28, 2017

Happy. Sad. Conflicted. Complicated. Content. Simple. Angry. Depressed. Thrilled. Ecstatic. Hysterical. Terrified. Trepidatious. Loving. Dramatic. These are only a handful of emotions that every person has, yet, with the advent of Pinterest quotes, Facebook updates, tweets and Instagram inspirational pages, we see day in and day out the mantra that we "only have room for positivity" in our lives. We come from a stoic society wherein our ancestors were taught to "Keep Calm and Carry On", and gradually, in North America, we learned to share and express our feelings. We are taught that sharing our thoughts is healthy, and healing. This, naturally, leads to something of which I am terribly guilty – the overshare. I am sure that the cult of positivity is a reaction to the rise of TMI (Too Much Information), but does that make it right? Is it fair to expect that no one ever expresses an emotion that is not outward cheerfulness and boundless energy?

We all have bad days, and sometimes we need to vent. In the world of social media, most often this involves a tweet stating that "ughhhhh! I have an awful case of Mondays!!" If this happens once in a while, the person is often told to cheer up, or that they are not alone; should this continue on to a terrible case of Friday FOMO (fear of missing out) the person's friends begin to roll their eyes and think they may need to unfollow the 'Debbie Downer'. The truth is that everyone needs to care for themselves, and when a person's negative moods begin to impact you, it is understandable to need to back away temporarily, but have we become so plastic that we feel it is desirable to have only happy, positive things in our lives? Why are we not allowed to be sad, or mad, or stressed?

Those who have read Aldous Huxley's Brave New World or have so much as seen Pixar's Wall-E, know that we can "positive" ourselves right into oblivion. Insomuch as negativity is handled in small doses, maybe it is time to remember that only having positivity in our lives does not make us grown-ups, in opposition to one image I saw today, stating that "as I grow older, I know that I need only happiness, positivity. I know that I don't have time for negativity or stress." We need all our emotions and feelings to be well-rounded. Pretending to be happy is not the antidote to stress, but rather the surest way to lose one's temper when the straw breaks the camel's back.

In the 1990s, we enjoyed angst. Musicians, filmmakers, clothiers, and amateur poets lived their sadness to the point of excess. At the turn of the millennium, we turned to sparkles and pop and colour. We have gorged ourselves on the desire to be happy. Who doesn't want to be happy? We all do. But that is not to the exclusion of anything not pleasant. I have seen far too many "inspirations" lately about only having happiness in one's life and knowing far too many people to whom this causes stress. We fear to share our stress or negativity, as we have seen our friends post "ain't nobody got time for that" time and time again.

If that is so, do we ever truly feel positive? Even the youngest child knows that these cannot be darkness without light. Moana faces Tefiti; women stand up for our rights; Americans stand in solidarity with their Muslim neighbours when unjust laws are written. Sometimes, there is stress, and sometimes, we feel negative. It is my belief that we need to embrace both.

"Actual happiness always looks pretty squalid in comparison with the overcompensations for misery. And, of course, stability isn't nearly so spectacular as instability. And being contented has none of the glamour of a good fight against misfortune, none of the picturesqueness of a struggle with temptation, or a fatal overthrow by passion or doubt. Happiness is never grand." — Aldous Huxley, Brave New World

MY SEMICOLON STORY:

THANK YOU, AMY BLEUEL

March 31, 2017

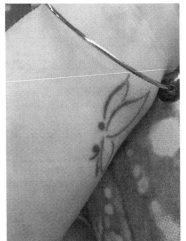

I have always hated tattoos. I have a fear of needles that is ironic for a person who has spent more than half of her life being poked. When I was married, I forced my sister-in-law to cover her tattoos with a bracelet and bridesmaid's dress, because "I hated tattoos" (bridezilla much??). So, what, you may wonder, am I doing with a butterfly semicolon tattoo on the inside of my left wrist? Why would someone who never, ever, ever, EVER wanted a tattoo spend perfectly good money on something like that?

Because I got sick. Again. At 7, I had a still-undiagnosed bout of fainting spells that had me in and out of specialists' offices, therapists, and even the hair salon, without ever finding out what caused them. At 13, I was diagnosed with Hashimoto's – it wasn't very well understood at the time, and the doctor couldn't even tell me how I had "contracted" it. I spent what felt like months, and months, and months of my life sick and undergoing tests. At 16, I had another long bout of illness that remained unexplained. My thyroid seemed fine, but I was simply sick. There was talk that maybe it was chronic fatigue syndrome, or maybe I was just a lazy teenager who didn't want to go to school. I stayed home and worked with a tutor, falling asleep over my textbooks and struggling to pass. At 21, I was depressed, and told that talk therapy would help. At 25, I suffered undiagnosed postpartum depression. At 27, my thyroid plummeted through my second pregnancy. At 29, I was miserable because my beloved grandfather was dying, and began over-exercising and undereating to control my body – the one thing I could control. I was seeing specialists because food literally caused me pain. My gallbladder was removed. I had a colonoscopy. I was diagnosed with IBS with severe food intolerances. At 32, my body gave up on me. I was in pain, I was depressed, I couldn't get out of bed. My thyroid levels swooped and plummeted. I thought I would die. I couldn't move, I couldn't care for my babies. I began to wonder if they wouldn't be better off if I just went away. I felt terribly lonely. I felt sick. I felt irritable. I felt angry. I felt scared. I spent so much time in the bath that I think the kids thought that I may have been part fish. My family rescued my kids and took care of them while I went to appointments, blood tests, slept, and cried.

During this last event, I remember clearly, sitting in my bathtub, looking at my wrists and thinking that if I could ever make it out of this alive, this would have been the hardest thing I had ever done, and I would need to permanently remind myself that I had done it before and could do it again. I knew it needed to be the one thing I swore I would never have, because given my history, there was a very good chance that eventually, I would find myself back to the point where getting dressed was a struggle and I needed my reminder to be in my skin, as much as my freckles and my moles are in my skin. I decided that I would need a tattoo.

When I was finally diagnosed with fibromyalgia, and began my regimen of Cymbalta, I felt so happy, so healthy, so well, so elated. It was the most amazing I could remember feeling for more than half of my life. I told my sister-in-law (the one whom I had forced to cover up her tattoos… Because mea culpa, and she knew good tattoos) that I needed a tattoo, and she was surprised. She asked me to really think about it. To make sure it was what I wanted. She knows me too well to think that I would never regret doing something I had always dug my heels in about. When it was clear that I really, really wanted a tattoo, she found me an amazing tattoo artist. I had my husband draw a butterfly on my wrist. Renewal, rebirth, and not coincidentally, the universal symbol for Thyroid Disease. I wanted a butterfly.

Then, while I was still working to decide how big I wanted my butterfly, if I wanted it in color, etc., and was thoroughly enjoying my newfound health and mental wellbeing, Amy Bleuel's Semicolon Project went viral on my social media. I am not one to do things because everyone else is, I wear leggings covered in the face of Benedict Cumberbatch; I stopped wearing my yellow fisher man's rain slicker when they came into popularity; I fumed when friends would go out and buy a piece of clothing that I owned. Being weird and unique is a big part of my personal identity, so it was not the trend of the Semicolon Project that spoke to me, it was Amy Bleuel's reason for creating it in the first place. It showed that a person could go through something terrible and make it a pause in her life, rather than a period, and the end of her life. A reminder that things can get better. Pause. Breathe. Keep going.

Now my butterfly needed a semicolon. I asked my husband to design it. I brought it to the artist, who put her own elegant touch on it, and my sister and dear friend took me for my tattoo. They both were tattooed first, in solidarity. I will always, always, always love them for that.

I am writing this today because Amy Bleuel came to the end of her sentence. At 31 years old, a woman who inspired so many of us that suffer mental illness, could no longer see that things would get better. She left the Earth on March 23, by suicide. It is with tears for a woman that I never knew that I share my Semicolon Story. And hopefully, by sharing our stories, Amy Bleuel's legacy will continue, and our stories will continue; after the pause.

MENTAL HEALTH AWARENESS

April 13, 2017

"Of course, it is happening inside your head, Harry, but why on earth should that mean it is not real?" ~ Albus Dumbledore (*JK Rowling – Harry Potter and The Deathly Hallows 2007*)

We commonly brush people with anxiety and depression off by telling them "it's just in your head". This does not help because that does not mean it isn't real to the person experiencing the panic or the loneliness. This line says so much for those suffering. Just because it is happening in your head does NOT mean it isn't real. You cannot escape your own mind, and therefore, without help, what is happening in your own head is terrifyingly real.

March 12, 2018

Ever vocal about mental health struggles, and an undeniable, wand-carrying member of the Harry Potter Fandom, this quote has long resonated with me as the epitome of what depression and mental illness can feel like. The shame associated with mental illness often derived from the societal belief that the pain one feels is not "real" because it is in one's head. Those of us who suffer are told to get over it because it's not real, we are imagining things and that we need to get passed it. The moment when I read these words, as uttered by beloved patriarchal figure Albus Dumbledore, I finally had a way to explain depression and mental anguish not just to myself, but to anyone who felt that my suffering and the suffering of millions was not a "real" problem. It's in my head, but that does not mean it isn't real.

I DON'T WANT TO TALK:

AN INTROVERT'S MUSINGS ON VOCALIZING

April 26, 2017

Do I want to talk? No, not really. Do I have things to say? Yes, of course.

I do not like out loud. I do not enjoy, nor have I ever enjoyed, talking on the phone. Sometimes, I will talk to my mom for an hour on the phone, and sometimes the idea of forcing words to come out of my mouth simply feels too exhausting. The words are there, floating around in my mind; I can taste them in my mouth, while my tongue stays firmly pressed against my palate, guarding against a burst of confidence or energy that will push the words out into the open. The words feel so much easier to share in written form. I think them – the fully formed sentences, the fragments, the commas, the quotes and quotation marks, and in text form, they are beautiful. They are my things to say.

The arrival of texting and social media in my life has been a freeing gift. It freed the things I have to say to circumvent the firmly held tongue and gives me the virtual pen my words needed to become verbalized. But not vocalized. Please not vocalized. My fear of speaking could be shyness, reticence, snobbishness, coolness: maybe it is all those things, but it is *also* utter anxiety and exhaustion. A bit like the Grinch with "the noise, oh the noise, noise, *noise,* **NOISE**!!", I do not care to add my voice to the noise. But I have thoughts and I was taught that the most important way our thoughts can be formed is to engage. So, I tweet, blog, Facebook, Instagram, text, email, Snapchat, write, read, share… and I *am* engaged. But no, I do not want to talk.

WORKING ON MY WISHES

May 1, 2017

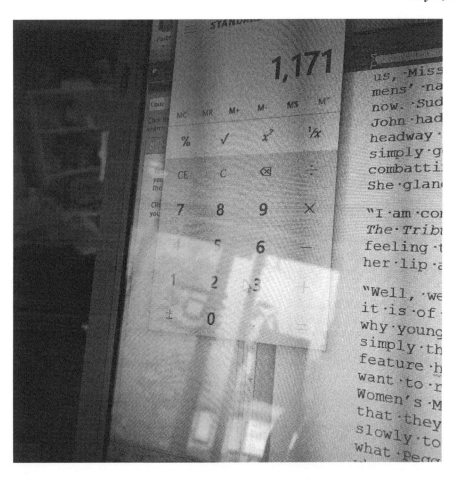

Dear sweet, funny Baby Kali – thinking that she would be writing that novel in 6 months. So full of ambition and hope and plans. Funny little thing. 3 years later, a husband with cancer, 2 job changes, COVID-19, and all the other billions of little things that make up the life that happens while we are busy making other plans. No clue. But you, dear reader, are getting to see the nuts and bolts of a life lived, with the benefit of hindsight. So, we shall be kind to Baby Kali's gentle heart. She didn't know better yet.

It is quiet for the moment, so I took an hour to myself. I set myself a daily goal of 600 words and am proud when I manage to smash it. I am really hoping to get this draft finished in the next 4 months, but I am only 42% of the way there…

The thing is that I have always wanted to do this, and yet, I have always convinced myself that I am not good enough, or that other people are better, or that my imagination is not imaginative enough, or at my worst – no one cares what you have to say. The thing is, it doesn't matter! Of course, some people are better than me, and who have wilder imaginations or do not care what I have to say. There are always people like that. Shakespeare wrote for the masses and is now considered literature; Fifty Shades of Grey started as fanfic and became a phenomenon. It does NOT matter. What matters is that I want to write. And the only way to fulfill my dream of being a writer is to write. Will this ever become a book with my name printed on the cover? I don't know. But it most certainly will not if it stays in my head. I won't win the lottery because I never buy a ticket, and I will never publish a book if the story stays in my mind.

So, 42% is better than 0% and if the first draft is finished in 6 months instead of 4, will it really matter? I don't think so.

GOODNIGHT, MY BOY

May 16, 2017

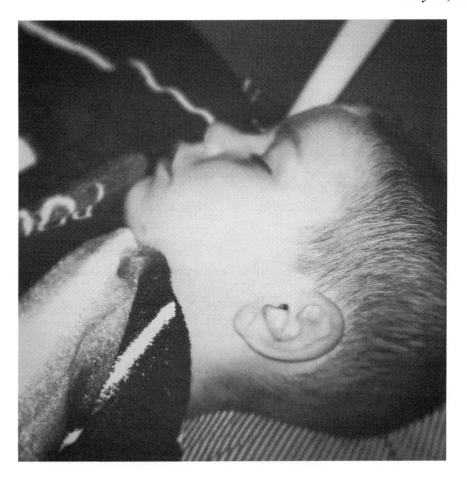

I am lying on my son's bed, waiting for his breathing to become regular and his ever longer body to relax back to sleep. He is seven and only in sleep do his features smoothen and soften enough for me to find the baby he was not more than two days ago. Right now, his thin body is taut with frustration, as he hates having his sleep disrupted. He awoke in tears, and as I rub his back and kiss his bristly head, shushing and whispering endearments to the sweet man child next to me. My exhausted brain wishes desperately to be in my bed, fast asleep, and it begs me to kiss him and tell him that I love him, and then slip out of the room to bed. But my heart keeps me here for just a little longer. In seven years he has grown from a small, pudgy cuddle bug into a wiry, long cuddle bug, and I know that seven years hence I will have a young man, who will likely be taller than me, and will more than likely no longer cry out for me in the night, no longer crave my closeness as a comfort. And so, I stay.

In the morning, my head will ache, and I will get ready for work in a daze, as I remember to give my daughter her antibiotics for a flaming ear infection, and my son will fight me, dragging his feet and not remembering why he feels so tired. I will kiss my kids as I leave them in the care of another woman who will ensure that they breakfast, and pack them off to school. And I will sit quietly on the train, drinking my home-brewed cup of tepid coffee, feeling tired and achy from my night of angling myself around this small, nearly sleeping form, but I will not regret the extra 20 minutes that I spent here. Because there is now, and now he will be grown, and then I shall miss the son that lies here right now, just as I miss his kindergarten, preschool, toddler, baby iterations. People talk of cutting into their sleep to get things done, and so that is what I am doing. I am gathering these moments and imprinting them on my memory, hoping that they will stay here, so that 35 years from now I will be lying in my bed and will be able to pull this out, dust it off and be with the seven-year-old who needed his Mama in the middle of the night.

A PLEA FOR PEACE:

IN HONOUR OF THE VICTIMS OF THE MANCHESTER BOMBING

May 23, 2017

My heart is heavy today. The hearts of the western world are heavy today. When someone walks into space primarily filled with children, with an improvised explosive device and sets it off, that is not an act of war, it is a statement. It forces us to examine how we allow our children to interact with the world, how we allow the freedom to grow when we fear that at any time, they can be taken from us. That is the statement terrorists want to make – be afraid, because no matter what you do or where you go, or your religious or political affiliation, we *could* be there. The name associated with such situations – a terrorist attack – has the word terror built right into it. A terrorist attack is also a two-part statement – first, there is the initial attack, the loss of life, the heartbreak; secondly, there is the terror, the fear, the suspicion. We see images on our screens of the perpetrator and begin to feel wary of people who look like that person, then it spreads, and we feel wary of all people not in our immediate circle. This fear allows us to begin to do the unthinkable – we begin to believe that we need to bring our own bombs to them, we need to send bombs to hurt them, and their children, and we are righteously angry because they killed our babies, our mothers, our cousins, our fathers. But then those whom we retaliate against, retaliate against us. And so, it goes.

I am angry. I am heartbroken. I want justice. But I do not want other children to die, to make up for these children who were so wrongly murdered. They deserve love and memories. A child loves unconditionally, they see the good in people, they smile, they laugh, and they make friends with other kids, without even knowing their names. They ought to be remembered through acts of love, and peaceful resolution to the conflicts brewing the world over.

I pray that the people who killed these children in Manchester last night are brought to justice. I pray that ISIS is dismantled, and I pray for peace. The 14th Dalai Lama, Nobel Peace Prize Winner, and the representation of the Buddhist philosophy of peace was driven from Tibet when China invaded and continues to offer peaceful solutions to end this conflict. He is quoted as having said "peace is not just the absence of violence, but rather the manifestation of human compassion", and to that end, I wish for us to find peace.

It is not enough to use bombs to stop bombs. It is not enough to be just as hateful as the man who walked into a building filled with innocent people and set off a suicide bomb. When we fight hate with hate, more innocents will be killed and more and more and more. It is time for those in power to create real solutions to the international tensions that are causing us to hurt each other. It is time for us, the citizens of the world, to demand peaceful resolution to these conflicts. It is time for us all to stop hiding behind whatever religious book we follow and see that at the heart of each of these texts, the core values are love, peace and acceptance. It is time for us to accept that leaders who have no interest in peace are not the leaders that we should have in a post-nuclear world.

Please let us find in our hearts the ability to solve these crises and heal our world because we do not want evil to win. We need peace. So, remember Manchester. Remember the faces of the victims, and let's honour them, by not adding more faces to the list of the dead.

"Hate has caused a lot of problems in this world, but it has not solved one yet."
~ Maya Angelou

WHY DO YOU CARE?

OUR SOCIETAL OBSESSION WITH BABY-MAKING

May 29, 2017

Have you ever known a childless (child-free?) woman of around 35 and had it pop into your head "is she ever going to get around to having kids?" Have you ever looked at a woman who has a great career, travels the world, is in a happy relationship, etc. and thought "she'll never be fulfilled until she has a baby of her own?" Yeah, I thought so. Can I ask you a direct question? Do you have kids? Oh, you do. Perfect, wonderful! Congratulations! That is the most beautiful baby/child/teen/adult I have ever seen. You must feel so fulfilled. So much so that you have made it your job to ensure that no woman alive misses out on *your* life. Have you travelled often? Oh no, I agree, travelling with kids is hard and expensive, best wait till they are older. Hey, can I ask you another question? Have you ever looked at a woman who has multiple children and thought "my god! She'll never get her life back at that rate!"? Yeah? What's your max? 3? 4? That's what I figured. But I am a little confused – if a woman cannot be fulfilled without kids, how can she then also have too many kids? Oh, wait, right… because she is a woman.

I have been feeling irked by recent discussions, articles and society in general, but today's ire is directed at people who think that a woman's baby making skill – wait, let's not even call it a skill, let's call it what it is – a natural ability that you have no control over – is the way to a happy and fulfilled life. I have many happy mom friends and many happy non-mom friends, and I would not say that one group feels fulfilled than the other simply by having pushed a human through their "birth canal". I would argue, though, that both feel unrelenting pressure with regards to their choices. But why?? Why do we as society care if a woman procreates or not? Not only is what a person does with their internal organs none of your damn business but because it points to a fatal flaw in our society: sexism. We are conditioned to think that motherhood is magical because if we don't, we won't want to do it. We are conditioned to talk to our friends and family into having a sweet adorable baby because babies smell so good. But why are we conditioned into thinking this? Babies smell so good, true (most of the time… the rest of the time they smell like a dirty diaper, sour milk, and some sort of sticky thing in their hair that you can't quite tell what it is…), however, that is not what has caused us to feel that we and every other female on the planet should make use of our uterus – we are meant to be carrying on the line. We are the protectors of our husbands' names. Without us, his family line could become extinct (regardless of whether he has 13 brothers, with sons of their own…).

Right now, Hulu has created a series based on Margaret Atwood's The Handmaid's Tale, and the idea of treating women as bags of fertility is in the fore. I have not seen the show, but I have read the original source material. In 1986, Atwood wrote a book wherein bit by bit women's rights were stripped away from them – including a country-wide mass firing of all women in the country because it became illegal for women to hold down a job. In Atwood's novel, a fertility crisis had broken out and all women with functioning uteruses were rounded up to make babies for the men to have, and for his infertile wife to raise. Yes, this is far-fetched, but at the microcosmic level, this is what we do when we try to convince every woman we ever meet that she ought to take up the reins of parenthood. Think about my earlier question – when you are speaking to your "woefully child-free" friend, how do you talk about motherhood? Do you tell the truth, the whole truth, and nothing but the truth, so help you, Universal Creator, of whom you may or may not believe? No. You talk about cuddles and baby's breath, and I Wuv Oo, Mamas. You talk about never having experienced love like this. When you talk to your mom friends, you talk about Tommy's inability to stop gnawing the furniture like a beaver, you talk about diarrhea and episiotomies. Do you know why? Because we mommies of the world are conditioned to be the saleswomen of our species. And we only share the fine print once you have bought in. When a child-free woman says she is tired and too busy, we are taught to roll our eyes and mutter under our breaths "you have no idea about busy until you have 1/2/3/4 kids. What are you complaining about?" It's ridiculous. Being a mother does not give you the monopoly on exhaustion! In a society where we are constantly connected, constantly reachable, and more often than not constantly connected to our jobs, how can a woman who works hard, yet doesn't have to rush to daycare, and is therefore tied to her desk for longer not allowed to be tired?

Being a woman is difficult. Being a mom is difficult. Being a non-mom is difficult, but back to my original point – if you were not conditioned to carry on the species, why would you care whether all your friends had babies or not? You wouldn't. So then – why do you care? It really is none of your business.

SCOTIABANK VANCOUVER MARATHON AND 5K

June 26, 2017

In 2012, I took up running. I loved it and began collecting finisher medals and the sense of joy from running outdoors. In 2014, I became so ill that running was no longer possible, and I would watch longingly as other people ran by. In 2015, my health began to improve, and I hoped far ahead to the day I could lace up my runners again. In 2016, my friend invited me to join her in the Donut Dash, and it was hard. I walked so much and mentally berated myself for what I had "lost". I kept going, and slowly added 15 mins here and there of running. On Mother's Day 2017, my mom presented me with a framed photo of me in a race that I had been particularly proud of years ago. And today, I ran my first 5K in years. There was walking thrown in, but for the most part, I was able to slowly jog along the Vancouver Seawall and cross the finish line, still running. I am so proud of myself! I am proud of this medal. And I am so very, very happy to be doing my sport again.

NO, I DO NOT WANT HER TO BE "LADYLIKE"

June 29, 2017

This morning, while driving my kids to out-of-school care, my 9-year-old daughter said from the backseat "Mama, why do I have to sit with my legs squished together?" A quick glance back showed me that she was wearing a sundress, so I told her it was because she was wearing a dress and she doesn't want to show her underwear. She replied, "but even when I wear pants I have to", to which I replied that, no, if her pants were not split at the crotch seam there was no reason for her to sit like that. And then she mentioned HER (I'm sure every mother has a child that when their name crosses our child's lips we shudder slightly at the mini-Mean Girl frenemy that we wished they didn't have. In this case, let's call her Anna).

"Anna says that even when I wear pants, I ALWAYS have to sit with my legs squished together, or I am not ladylike. She said being not ladylike is rude," my daughter sounded confused as to why Anna would tell her one thing and her mommy would tell her something else…(just wait, my darling, you are only at the beginning of Mama disagreeing with your friends! We haven't even hit the teen years yet…)

Suppressing the desire to roll my eyes (after all, I am the grown-up here…*scary*), I said "if she says anything like that again, tell her that your mommy doesn't believe in ladylike. It is sexist and silly, and as long as you are not wearing a dress or a skirt, there is no reason to not sit however you feel comfortable". I explained to her that no one tells her brother to sit "ladylike", so why should she?

It made me think about how we indoctrinate our little girls from such a young age to be little "ladies" in more ways than just the pink, plastic Barbie way. (Case in point – one of my friends found pink Wonder Woman gardening gloves and tools… Wonder Woman does not wear pink, so why the colour choice? Little girls are perfectly capable of liking gardening gloves in Wonder Woman red, blue and gold!!) It may seem innocuous to tell our daughters to be ladylike, but it is a way of controlling their behaviour and teaching them to yield to gender norms. By teaching them that if they aren't ladylike, they are being rude we are limiting them to two options – a feral ruffian child, or a polite little girl. It is a way to strip their equality away before they even realize it – their brothers jump and shout and kick and run, and we say "oh he's such a boy!"; the girls try to jump and shout and kick and run, and we say "hush now! That's not ladylike!" We tell them to sit quietly, we tell them to dress prettily, we tell them to brush their hair, and keep their clothes clean, we tell them to be like princesses, we teach them to be little ladies. And it needs to stop.

So, I say no. My daughter is never as beautiful to me as when she is unkempt and freckled and free. When her eyes are bright, her head tipped back in a loud laugh; when she stands on the seawall facing the great Pacific Ocean, hair and dress whipping in the wind, arms flung back and her face peaceful. She does not need to be packaged to suit the norms of her gender. She needs to be kind, accepting of all people, polite, willing to stand up for herself and for others. She needs to express herself, and be allowed to be herself, just the same way that her brother can be. So please, do not tell our daughters to be ladylike. Do not pose them prettily, as though they were dolls. Do not ask them to keep their dresses tidy. Teach them to be strong, and brave, and truly and utterly themselves. Let them sit however they please and voice their opinions and explore; get dirty and loud and jump, and not keep their "legs squished together".

BUT I'M A FEMINIST...

July 4, 2017

My husband and I, on our wedding day (2006)

"I to know more about you! I see your profile and I adore you!" – complete strangers

Since setting up my blog and public Instagram account for my book reviews, I have received countless private messages from men whom I do not know, professing a desire to know my age, marital status and whether I would be DTF. I had originally thought that all these people were simply bots, and were set up to troll the internet, and my sites had just gotten in the way. However, now I am not confident that this is the case for every one of them.

I received an email through the address created specifically for my review site – for this blog – that told me that this person was a successful businessperson, and he was not successful in his personal life and would like to get to know me better. I do not usually respond to these sorts of messages, as they do not pertain to the topic of the blog. However, this day, I was particularly full of piss and vinegar and decided to reply. I told him I was sorry about his lack of success in his personal life, and that I reviewed books, and that that was what my profile told him. He replied that he knew this but would like to know me better than that. I told him there was not much else to know, and who was he? So, he suddenly became a single, tragic Roman banker, who travels the world for business and is currently settled in New York and was looking for someone to talk to. If you know me, you know that I absolutely hate small talk, and have no interest in carrying on ridiculous conversations with people that I am not even convinced exist. So, I did what I always do when I feel cornered by this type of person – I play the Married Card.

I have been married to my husband for nearly eleven years, we have been together for 18 years, we have two beautiful kids, and the fact that our relationship is still going strong is one of my proudest accomplishments; HOWEVER, I am also a feminist who has only recently felt brave enough to use my voice loudly and publicly, and now I feel that the old go-to shield of my wedding ring is not very feminist at all. Why should I allow the fact that my husband exists be the reason that I do not care for unwanted advances and flirtations? I don't want them because they are rude, they are uncalled for, they are disgusting, and I am a human being who ought to be treated like one. The man who messaged me last week saying that he "came across [my] gorgeous profile" and wanted to know what I do said that he doesn't care for books – the direct message came through my Bookstagram profile. When I told him, I reviewed books and what sort did he like, he replied "I don't read, but I just "adore you"". What sort of nonsense is this? What part of book reviews gives you the impression that I want you to hit on me?

In the months since this blog has been live, I have been woken to a whole new world of male privilege – if a profile looks female, I shall hit on her, and she shall be honoured! I have friends who are single and deal with this sort of crap in "real life", and this furthers my desire to break free of my easy reply of "married" – they do not have that to go to when a situation gets uncomfortable. I have had friends turn down dates because they weren't interested to have the men lash out via text that they were not deserving of love or attention; I have had friends find their dating stories show up online and themselves dehumanized. Male entitlement and privilege are a thing in real life, but when we are just typing, we, as people, feel safer to spew nastiness or innuendo than we would in person. I wonder if some of these messages would be spoken aloud should these people meet me in the street. I wonder if my friends' would-be paramours would be so quick to switch to nasty name-calling or depersonalizations if my friends had been sitting across the table?

I wish I had a suggestion or a closing argument that would cause these things to stop. I wish there was a button next to the mute button on my Twitter that said "Chauvinist". I wish my friends did not have their own insecurities thrown back in their faces by these men. And most of all, I wish… no, I am DETERMINED to defend myself and shut people down without making my "man" do it for me.

CELEBRATING THE ANNIVERSARY OF THE MEAN REDS

July 12, 2017

July 11, 2014 – do you remember what you were doing that day? Would you remember what you did if Facebook didn't force the highlights of what you liked or shared that day? I do. I can tell you exactly what I was doing that day. It was a hot, sunny day. My extended family was descending upon my grandmother's retirement facility to release butterflies in memory of my Grampa, who had succumbed to pancreatic cancer a year and a half earlier. After the release, I was leaving my daughter with my mom and sisters and was taking my son to an appointment at the hospital. I was then going to drive back to my mom's house to pick up my daughter and rejoin my family for a barbecue. It was a busy schedule, but as a stay at home mom, it was a typical day.

During the butterfly release, I kept feeling overheated and needed to sit down or lean on the wall. I thought I was coming down with a cold or was simply too worn out by the emotional day. I could barely muster up the energy to smile when my nephew, one of my favourite people in the world, told me his butterfly had kissed his cheek. I then drove my son half an hour back to our town hospital. I could feel my heart racing and began to worry that I should not be driving. I thought it was odd that I was so anxious about the non-invasive tests that the hospital would be running on my five-year-old son. When we pulled into the parking lot at the hospital, I was so anxious and hot that I sincerely wished I could have slipped out of my skin and into something cooler. I opened the windows and sat in the car, with my son, hoping that the feeling of anxiety, heat and the subsequent racing heart, shallow breathing and confusion, would pass and my son and I would be able to continue with our busy day.

It didn't pass. While waiting for my son's exams, I messaged my mom and my husband and told them something was wrong. I told them my husband would need to pick our daughter up, and that I needed to go home. I told my mom that I thought there was something wrong with my thyroid, as I was shaking so much. At 13, I had been diagnosed with Hashimoto's Hypothyroidism, and had lived the subsequent 18 years listening carefully to what my body was telling me, and when it didn't think it was getting enough of the Thyroid Stimulating Hormone (TSH). I did not feel "hypo", as that presented, in me, like lethargy, exhaustion, confusion, coldness and depression. This felt "hyper". My mom understood and arranged to have my daughter brought home. When my son and I went home, it was all I could do to make it up the jack and the beanstalk-sized staircase (I could have sworn it was a regular staircase that morning…) and crawl into my bed.

I laid there, my body shaking so badly that I could feel my bed moving. I did what I always do when I feel lousy – I called my mommy. I told her what was going on, and she agreed that it was not good. She asked me if I needed anything and I said no. She did not agree and called my husband and suggested that he come home and told him that I was in a bad way.

That was The Day I Got Sick. Again. This time, I was a grown woman with two little kids who needed care. This time, I was a grown woman who would need to figure this out. This time, I could not convalesce in my bedroom plastered with Jonathan Taylor Thomas posters, while my mom ran interference with the doctors and my responsibilities. Or so I thought. My parents and sister, sister-in-law, and friends showed up for me in the biggest way. My parents took the kids to stay with them most of every week, all summer. My kids had fun, though I felt guilty that they would feel they had been abandoned by their Mama. They did not feel abandoned, they were having a blast, but I still felt guilty.

The year that followed July 11, 2014, was one of the hardest of my life – I went to every specialist under the sun, had blood tests weekly, and could barely praise myself out of bed to get my kids to school. I had to explain to both of their teachers why they were consistently late for school, and to please direct their annoyance at me, and not at the kids.

It was hard and awful, and I truly felt that this was the worst period of my life. The doctors didn't know what was wrong with me, and therefore couldn't tell me when or if I would ever feel better. My life was figuratively paused, while those of my friends and family carried on.

July 11, 2015 – after a diagnosis of fibromyalgia, and treatment that helped, my sister and her best friend took me to get a tattoo. It was one year to the day of the

Day I Got Sick, and I wanted to commemorate my survival and health with a permanent reminder that I was stronger than I thought I was.

July 11, 2017 – to mark the third anniversary of The Day I Got Sick, I went to exercise with one of my amazing friends that texted with me through it all. As I did squats and lunges, and whatever other forms of private hell we could think of, I inwardly beamed. I am not as strong, or as fit, or as thin as I was in 2014, but I am infinitely happier. As I put my body through its paces, I was gentle with myself and relished the fact that three years ago, I would not have been capable of doing any of this. The Mean Reds are gone, (most of the time) and my body and I are working towards a delicate trust. There is something so exhilarating about regaining lost health and being able to swing a kettlebell, regardless of how light it is when in recent memory, I could not even swing my legs out of bed.

GIVE

July 25, 2017

My province is in an official state of emergency. There are so many forest fires and so many evacuees that the entire province is in crisis. A full fire ban is in effect. If you are caught around an open flame, not just the person who started the fire, but all those around the fire will be ticketed. If you are caught throwing a cigarette out your car window, you may have it impounded. Companies and individuals are working around the clock to gather money, supplies, and resources. People are opening their homes to the evacuees, preparing cots and air mattresses for those fleeing the disaster. British Columbians are coming out in force to help our neighbours. This makes me proud. I believe, sometimes to my own detriment, and often to the consternation of my husband, that if I have something, I have something to give. I have been known to stick a $20 bill into a fireman's boot, even though that is the last $20 I have at my disposal. I have "adopted" children in Third World countries; I have added money to my grocery bill for kids to get books in schools; at a previous job, I faced my insane fear of heights to sit on the roof of the grocery store I worked in, to raise money for BC Children's Hospital. This is not to make me sound like Mother Theresa. I'm not. I am just as self-centred and mean as the next person, but it is simply to demonstrate that giving is not something I avoid doing. I read a passage in Trevor Noah's book *Born A Crime* where he says that instead of giving a man a fish or teaching him to fish, we need to also give him a fishing pole to be able to fish. That strikes me as apt: what good is knowing how to fish, if you can't afford to buy the tools to catch the fish? I do not believe that giving charity is wrong; I do not believe in everyone for themselves. I believe in giving.

Tonight, a well-known charitable organization (globally, not just in BC) came to my door in the form of a charming young Irish man. If you know me, you know that I am a sucker for an accent, so I was content to let him explain why he was there. He asked me if I would be able to sign up to give $30 a month to help those affected by the fires. He made a joke that $30 a month won't have me living in a tent on the street. I told him that unfortunately that it was more than I could afford now and was there another option for donating. He said that the website is always available but rolled quickly into a spiel about how that wasted valuable dollars by paying an administration fee that would otherwise go to relief. And then told me it was better to just sign up with him. I began to feel guilty and uncomfortable because my desire would be to simply say yes, and sign up for it, but due to financial issues of my own, I simply don't have that much extra money, while caring for my kids. I told him I am sorry, but I really couldn't commit to that and thanked him for what he was doing for the victims. He then said "c'mon! What're 4 quarters a day? The rest of your neighbours have given,

you've got a generous neighbourhood. It's true what they say about Canadians being nice! You need to continue the trend and be just as generous as your neighbours!" He continued to needle me in a cheerful way, and I continued to feel guilty, but simply could not say yes to this. I know that there are other ways to help, ways that I can afford, while still contributing. I reiterated that no, I'm sorry, but I would not be able to. He then asked me why I resisted, and feeling the flush of humiliation, while standing in the doorway of my own home, I clumsily explained that due to financial matters, I could not spare that much a month. Then he asked for a void cheque, saying it would give me time to save up before the cheque was processed, and that it would be easy to cancel if need be. I could not believe this: I had finally mustered up the ability to say no, and I was being not only
ignored, but pressured and made to feel like I was making a bad decision. I felt so ashamed at not being able to help, and frustrated that he continued to push, while unable, due to some ingrained sense of politeness to close the door on him. The kicker for me, was that when my husband stepped in and said "I believe my wife already said no", the young man stepped back, put his hands up and said "of course, yes, I do not mean to pressure", and left quickly.

We all want to help. Ok, well, almost all of us want to help. It is natural to want to help our fellow humans. I believe this strongly and shake my head when I hear Randian me, myself and I arguments. I appreciate that I am an easy mark because of this. My own sense of guilt at not helping, my people-pleasing tendencies and my difficulty with saying "No" are all blindingly obvious to those looking for someone to subscribe to a fund. What I do not appreciate is that to be taken seriously, my husband needed to step in. My no is the same as his no. My money and his money coexist quite happily in their mutual bank account. My budget and his budget are the same. We are both looking to feed and cloth our shared children. Yet his no is respected instantly, and mine is poked and prodded and harangued.

At this point, some of you can see where I am going with this, and are thinking "seriously? How did she make a post about the state of emergency in British Columbia into a feminist issue??" Well, folks, I'm glad you asked. *I* did not make it a feminist issue. The young man representing a global charity and relief fund made it a feminist issue when he demonstrated that to him what a woman says is not as valuable or as true as what a man says. I am home from work sick with bronchitis and a sinus infection, I can barely speak, and yet, I could not end the conversation with this fellow. My husband walks into the room, and he is gone within 15 seconds. This, my friends, is *exactly* why we still need feminism. Therefore, I will repeat myself like a broken record. Therefore, I will stand on my virtual soapbox. When my croaky sick voice is taken with the same seriousness as that of my husband, then I will step down, but not a moment sooner.

*seriously, though, if there is anything you can do to help those affected by the fires in BC, please donate. Whatever you can do, even spare some of your time, can make a difference.

WINTER BRINGS THE DARK

December 10, 2017

Where have I been? I have been hibernating. I have been curling into myself. I have been napping. I have been working. I have been hiding. I have spoken about my anxiety and depression in the past, so this is nothing new. Nothing insightful. Simply a confession that I have been picking myself back up. I have learned that even the most powerful medicine and deepest desire cannot keep that darkness completely away. Overwhelming, exhausting, imposing, intrusive. Depression doesn't "go away" I am not cured. It will always be there, lurking. Sometimes, though, it steps forward – it reminds me at times when I need the least reminding that it is still a part of me and beckons me to curl up under a heavy blanket and let it fog my brain over. In the interest of taking control, I made significant changes over the last months. I left environments that caused me pain, I found a peaceful space to rebuild and have found my foundations firming up again. The crumbling is plastered over and has abated. I am mitigating my loss. My lifelines are firm, seeing me slip back, they reached out and pulled me gently back out of the darkness. And tonight, with tea, a hot bath, a sweet candle and my dear, dark Joan Didion, I can feel my depression slip back, and my hope ebb forward once again.

MOTIVATION MONDAY

(Because what self-respecting blog doesn't have at least one Motivation Monday post?)

January 30, 2018

Motivation Monday – it is never too late to try. Don't give up your dream because you haven't gotten there yet. Now is as good a time as any.

Right about now, many of us are quickly scrolling past gym appointments that we meticulously logged on January 1st. Skittles are creeping back into the pantry. We are finding ourselves "too cold/too late/too tired" to park at the far end of the parking lot. The book that we were going to start writing has yet to be outlined. That's right, it is almost a full month since we made our resolutions for 2018.

But who cares if we have not stuck to our resolutions?? Who cares if we are a few weeks behind? Who cares that we missed the sign up for the dance class we planned to try?? Does that mean we have to throw away our goals for the next 11 months?? Does it mean we shake our heads, fully slip back into old patterns and give up? No!!

New Year's Day is an arbitrary beginning. What is the difference, in the grand scheme of things between January 1st and March 1st? January 1st and January 31st? Nothing! There is not a fracking difference, and thereby, I arbitrarily declare that those of us who have not fallen headfirst in love with our New Year's resolutions will begin today. Because today is as good a day as any to try!!

INTERNATIONAL WOMEN'S DAY!

March 8, 2018

It is International Women's Day 2018. This day means so much to me, not only as a feminist in the bell hooks-defined tradition but as a woman raising children to be successful, proud, fundamentally good people. I was raised to believe that in Canada, I was equal and that I didn't have to worry about civil rights like "they" did in other parts of the world. There was no longer a need for feminism, there was no longer racism… and I believed this. I went to university, believing that this was true. I truly thought that we were all equal. I was wrong. That was my privilege. Being a white-appearing, cisgender, heteronormative female, in a socialist country, with married, successful parents who provided me with a good education, I did not face the challenges that impact women in Canada and globally, for the most part. I thought stereotyping, and gender expectations and a lifelong virgin/whore moral fear was just part of womanhood. I was assaulted, I was catcalled and told to take it as a compliment and that that was just something women had to deal with. I was constantly anxious. I was depressed and fearful, I assumed that I would be attacked anytime I was alone. And then I woke up. I woke up to the realization that while I lived a sheltered, Anglo-Christian, Canadian life, this was not the reality for most women. I woke up to the realization that a stranger grabbing me in public was not a cause for me to feel ashamed. I woke up to the realization that being perfect was unrealistic. I woke up to the realization that maintaining my virginity until my wedding night was not something to be proud of – it was a patriarchal construct to ensure that women were denied a sexual self and that created further shame surrounding sex. I woke up to the realization that I would be raising small humans that would look to me to learn how to act and how to treat others. Most importantly, they would look to me to see how they should allow themselves to be treated. I needed to revaluate my thoughts. I needed to turn my shame, depression, fear and moral insecurity into action, advocacy and global citizenship. And so, I am trying. I am doing my best. And I am honouring women.

THANK YOU, EMMA GONZÁLEZ

March 25, 2018

Today, a little girl was the most mature woman in the world. Allow me to rephrase – the most mature *person* in the world. Emma González, a high school senior, stopped the world for 6 minutes and 30 seconds. Between her impassioned words and her silence heard 'round the world, Ms. González said more than any adult in America today. March For Our Lives, a global protest of gun violence and the epidemic that is mass shootings in the United States of America, took place today, as children took to the streets all over the world to demand their basic human right to life. As is our wont, humanity has shown itself to be divided on the issue of gun control, with a faction on the side of control, and a faction on the side of the "right" to bear arms. In my heart of hearts, I truly, concretely believe that the right to live outweighs the right to own a weapon that can cause such devastation. I do not intend to debate gun control, versus banning guns, versus the freedom to treat every problem like a showdown at the OK Corral. I simply want to state that I hope that one day, I can grow up to be half as brave, half as strong, half as fierce and half as brilliant as a young woman half my age. Thank you, Emma González, for taking to task those who do not care to protect you; do not take the time to understand that the gun lobby does not deserve your sympathy; thank you for your bravery, and thank you for stopping the conversation for 6 minutes and 39 seconds so that the world stopped to hear you. And I sincerely hope that we all heard her loud and clear.

THIS YEAR, I LEARNED THAT I DON'T HATE POETRY.

April 8, 2018

"The teacher said silence is golden/I said silence is bronze, at best" – Andrea Gibson *Take Me with You*

I fantasized about being a poet. I dreamed that I had a poetic bone. I read and read and read and read and hoped to fall in love with the poetic word, as I loved the prosaic. I never did. I read the words, and tried to reach them, but could not grasp them. I could not hold them and examine them, turning them over in my hands until I understood them.

I determined that though I longed to understand Byron, Shelley, Keats, and Dickinson, I was simply not romantic. I did not into poetry and that was that. I learned to read poetry with the same interest and gusto that I applied to read the periodic table of elements. (*read – little to none) I learned to circumvent the poetry section in libraries and bookshops for 20 years.

I simply did *not enjoy poetry*.
… the funny thing with definitive statements is that they are never truly definitive.

This winter, as I described in a previous post, I inadvertently purchased Sabrina Benaim's beautiful collection *Depression & Other Magic Tricks*, and for the first time, felt the poetry speak not around me, but to me. Benaim's words were for me and of me. How could this be? How could words along meters speak to me? There were no sentences, hanging pronouns, rules of grammar shattered. But I understood them.
… I tricked myself. I began to renegotiate my path through the bookstore, to *stumble* upon the stacks of poets. I flipped through them as I stood, waiting for my son to finish typing *Dog Man* into the computer at Chapters, glancing away from him briefly to read what words I had opened to.

I *understood* these words. Frowning, I flipped to another page and felt the same connection. I looked at the cover of Andrea Gibson's *Take Me with You* and saw that they were, in fact, a poet. I picked up another poet from the shelf and read that one, and that one, and that one. I *enjoyed* the poetry. *I enjoyed* the poetry. *I enjoyed the* poetry. *I enjoyed the **poetry***.
… the thing with declarative statements is that they often need to be retracted.

I may not enjoy Byron, Shelley, Keats, and Dickinson, but as it turns out, *I quite like poetry*, Sam-I-am.

I MIGHT BE A WEIRD MOM…

BUT I'M YOUR MOM

April 23, 2018

I am the mom who goes to the grocery store in a TARDIS onesie; the one who doesn't always brush her own hair, let alone ensure my kids are in matching socks; the one that tells her son that the reason he feels embarrassed to get a manicure is toxic masculinity, and sticks him in a feminist T-shirt from the time he can pronounce the word. I am the mom who takes her kids to see Avengers movies if Benedict Cumberbatch is them because… I don't think I need to explain that…; the mom who has more laundry than can have possibly been used in the last 3 months; the mom who thinks that having a stack of books in every corner of the house is actually good for her kids; the mom who will sit down to read a book rather than mop her kitchen floor every. single. day. of. the. week. I am the weird mama who wears gold sequins chucks because she has them, a TARDIS headband for her best friend's wedding, because why wouldn't I? The mom who buys Women of NASA LEGO because it is awesome; the mom who doesn't care if her kid wants to know what mayonnaise feels like; the mom who thinks singing Disney songs is important but is against the patriarchal ideals that sublimate the princess stories. And I am not in the least bit ashamed. If my kids learn anything from their weird mom, I want them to know that they can be themselves and that they need to speak their truths and they need to stand up for their beliefs. If they want pink hair, go for it. If they want to wear superhero capes every single day, go for it. I want their weird mama to teach them that shame is pointless, human rights are non-negotiable, and that there is ALWAYS time for nonsense.

MY KID IS AWESOME:

A NOT-SO-HUMBLE PROUD MAMA MOMENT

May 9, 2018

I have a 10-year-old daughter. She is everything that I could have ever hoped for in a little girl – she is silly, affectionate, funny, shy, dramatic, brave, beautiful, amazing. But the attribute that I find the most incredible is her empathy. Don't misunderstand – she can be just as selfish, and self-absorbed as every other child on the planet; she is not a sainted child, but she has an empathetic streak a mile wide.

When she was about 3, I remember her coming into the bathroom, after I had put her to bed. It had been a long, loooooong day. The kind where my one-year-old son was climbing up the walls (literally), my daughter was exerting her independence by resisting everything I did. The kind of day when, as a stay-at-home mom, I felt bone-crushingly tired. I was soaking in a no-longer-hot bath when she slid open the bathroom door, and my first instinct was "ugh! Why is she up again?? Why won't she just go to sleep??" She quietly looked at my face, walked to the edge of the tub and smoothed my hair off of my forehead, and said, in her baby lisp, "It's hard bein' Mama sometimes, isn't it?" and she just looked at me with her big blue eyes, and her wild hair crazy around her little face. I thought "wow. I made this?? This intuitive little being is actually mine?"

Since that night, I have found so many instances of her compassion and love for people. During a snowfall, she saw a man living under an overpass and she asked if we could bring him to our home since he didn't have one and bridges aren't very warm. At school, she befriends kids with special needs and doesn't even flinch at the idea of including them in her birthday parties. She has asked if she could make "like, a bunch, you know like FORTY pancakes and put them on plates" and bring them to the homeless camp in our city for Christmas breakfast. She understood when our neighbour's son, who is older than her, didn't know how to talk to her, because "it's just his way, Mama. We just keep being nice to him, and he will be ok". She was right.

Today, after a frustrating day, I picked the kids up from daycare, and with a car full of groceries, conjunctivitis and muscles still achy from my run on Sunday, I let them pick what they wanted for dinner. McDonald's. As we waited in the drive-thru, we noticed a man standing at the edge of the parking lot, with a sign that said "homeless. Hungry. Please help." I could see in the rear-view mirror that my girl was watching to see what he was doing. She didn't seem anxious, as I had been at her age, with the idea of a homeless man being nearby. She was thoughtful and curious. Then she said, "Mama, that man looks hungry, doesn't he?" I agreed. We have a significant homeless epidemic in our city, and this type of thing, a hungry, dirty-clothed *person* at a street corner begging. Then she said "did you know you overpaid my teacher for my field trip? She gave me some change. She gave me two dollars and some cents to give you back". She met my eyes in the rear-view mirror and said, "you know how you say as long as you have something, you have something to give"?" I said yes and asked her if she wanted to give him the change. She nodded emphatically and told me the money was in her backpack in the trunk. I parked the car and she jumped out to find the change. A young woman nearby saw what my girl was up to and asked if she would give the man $5 from her as well. She ran straight up to him, no fear, no anxiety, smiled and handed him the money. I could see them talk for just a moment before she ran back to the car. She said that she told him that $7 and some cents should be able to get him some food at McDonald's, so he wouldn't be hungry. She smiled to herself and watched as he rounded the corner. I asked her what the man had said to her, and she said, "he said he hoped I had a very, very, **very** nice day, and that I was kind, and he said thank you four times". I asked her if she was proud of herself, and she said she was. She was happy to have helped him, a little bit. Because that's her. That's her big soul in her little body. She wants to change the world, to make it a kinder, gentler, fuller place for everyone who lives here.

MOTHER'S DAY THOUGHTS

May 14, 2018

It's Mother's Day in Canada today. I spent the day with and celebrating some incredible women, both moms and maternal surrogates (non-moms who project the maternal instinct of love to their friends and families). While I celebrated, I was also thinking about how crazy motherhood is. I read a lot… I know, it's a shock, but try to keep your mind from being blown… and in some of my books, I find a lot of emphases placed on finding the root of our behaviours; often, the roots are seeded in childhood, for good or for bad. This leads to a whole discussion on whether one's mother was distant or overbearing, a tiger mom or a flake if she was open about sex or insisted that sex before marriage was terrible, if your mother played favourites, or made mistakes, or, or, or… What is not often discussed, other than in parenting books aimed at making us feel better as moms that we are not completely screwing our kids up, is the fact that becoming a mother does *not* suddenly bestow us with ancient maternal wisdom that will allow us to know how to handle every situation that comes our way. We are still the same women we were before we gave birth, just now with a new responsibility.

When my grandmother gave birth to her first child, she was 19 years old and had been married for 11 months. (I did the math for you…) When my mother gave birth for the first time, (me) she was 22 years old. I don't know about you, but I would not say that my problem solving and wisdom skills kicked until much later than 19 or 22. When I was 19, I was suffering through my first depressive episode, while I struggled to learn Portuguese at University (Não, I still do not speak Portuguese). When I was 22, I was panicking about graduating from university and desperately hoping my boyfriend of 6 years would propose to me. These are not the mindsets of a woman set to instil sage thoughts into the mind of another human. Today, there is a discussion that adulthood does not truly begin until at least the mid-twenties, but possibly as late as our 30s

My mom did a wonderful job raising my brother, sister and me. She raised creative individuals with a drive to succeed in whatever our chosen calling should be. My sister is a Ph.D. student, and single mother, adeptly handling both;

my brother is the COO of a major tech company. As the saying goes – the kids are alright. That said, whenever I am expected to confront my anxieties, fears, neuroses, depression, etc., I am directed to consider what might have occurred in my childhood to make me behave the way that I do. So, on this Mother's Day, as a mother, allow me to call Bull sh*t on this being the ONLY or
rather PERVADING reasons why I am a neurotic loon. I am not saying that I do not believe that events in our past cause us to be the way that we are – they do, and I am not saying that moms do not mess up their kids – we do; what I AM saying is on this Mother's Day, consider cutting your mom some slack. She literally did the best she could (*please be aware that I am not referring to abusive, neglectful, or malicious women. I am referring to the moms who tried, and yet couldn't always get it right).

When we were little,
we GENUINELY believed that our Mommies knew EVERYTHING. They were the most beautiful, the most amazing, the most perfect beings in the universe, and it was imperative that every question that popped into our heads be spewed directly at her, where she would immediately answer with a witty, cunning, intelligent response, lighting our way
to ALSO knowing everything, just like mommy.

When we got a bit older, we realized that sometimes, *maybe*, Mommy didn't seem to know exactly everything, because, after a few years at school, we came to realize that "because I said so" was not *actually* a suitable response to questions, and neither was "to make little girls ask questions".

When we became teenagers, many of us suddenly felt that these beacons of light, fun and beauty where actually old fussy ladies out to keep us from having fun. (I'll admit that that wasn't my belief, as I was born an old fussy lady, intent on stopping myself from having fun. I am pretty sure my mom would have encouraged a bit more fun on my part, had she had the chance.)

When we are older still, we begin to believe that our moms are not nearly as clever as we are, and how is it possible that *my mother* could not recite Clause 7 of the Canadian Charter of Rights and Freedoms, 1982? I mean she was
literally *alive* when that was signed!! (For the record, Section 7 states that "Everyone has

the right to life, liberty and security of the person and the right not to be deprived thereof except in accordance with the principles of fundamental justice".) Then we become adults and realize that between seeing her brilliance, and her flaws, our mom has become a fully actualized human, with her own pains, fears and anxieties. She may not have been made of sunbeams and rainbows, but by god, she knew how to get a stain out of a white shirt *even if it had a black trim*!!! She knew how to make a dinner for 5 plus any neighbourhood kids that stayed with essentially nothing in the fridge. She knew when we needed our heads stroked until 2AM, even though she had to get up for work tomorrow, as we cried our eyes out about a C on a math test.

But *how did she know how to do that???* When I was placed in my mom's arms at 22, she had no basis of comparison; she had no way of knowing if what she was about to do next, either by plan or by instinct, was the right thing for me. She had no idea whether she was setting me up for success or for failure, all she knew was that she loved me, and she was willing to try her best. When my grandmother was 19, and had a baby girl, and was preparing to move from the Prairies to the West Coast, she had *no idea* how she would manage. She had no idea how to keep a baby alive, but she knew she had to and that she loved my mom. (And in her case, she didn't even have the benefit of automobile safety!)

With my kids, I have no idea if I am screwing them up for life. I have no idea if I am involved enough, or too distant. I have no idea if I am projecting the image of a confident woman for them to model. I have no idea how to tell my daughter to make friends at school, or to not worry so much, because *I don't know how to make friends or not worry!!* All that I know is that I love her, and I want the best for her. And that every day, I will keep trying.

… and that, god-willing, when she inevitably reads something that tells her that all of her adult problems are rooted in my inability to parent correctly, she will see me as a whole person, who had a great responsibility, no training, and was just doing my best.

Happy Mother's Day to all the moms of the world, who are secretly just regular human beings and have no idea whether what we are doing is right. I am right there with you. □

A SAD AND EYE-OPENING WEEK:

MENTAL HEALTH AWARENESS

June 8, 2018

If this week of high-profile suicides does not shed light on the necessity to end the stigma of mental illness, I do not know what will.

We are "shocked" and "saddened" by the "sudden and unexpected death" of famous individuals, Kate Spade and Anthony Bourdain, but in our daily lives, we either do not speak of these issues or send out regular, often unconscious, microaggressions about mental illness. Rolling our eyes when someone is too depressed to join us for drinks at a bar; refusing sick days for anxiety-related issues; referring to mental illness as weakness or a personal failing… all of which promote the stigma that keeps those of us with mental illness firmly shut within our own dark, terrifying thoughts. Even suicide is called selfish and shameful. Therefore, when a mentally ill person is shut off from society, due to social cues, told that their pain is "in their heads", asked what they could POSSIBLY have to worry/be sad about, trapped in the prison of their brains, and then told that they are selfish for contemplating suicide, it is no wonder that suicides occur. This person feels that there is literally no other option and that they are unnecessary and unneeded, and that as selfish or as shameful as suicide may be, the world is better off without them. This is never the case, but they do not know this if we do not TELL them!!!

We need to open the dialogue about mental illness more often than when the worst happens. We need to let people know that they are valued and that we are listening. We need to make suicide prevention part of our ongoing social discourse. We need to stop being shocked and saddened and we need to start being proactive and humane.

WHEN WILL MENTAL HEALTH BE AS OPENLY DISCUSSED AS PHYSICAL HEALTH?

June 9, 2018

I have a stomach bug today. I have a fever and chills; I have been in and out of the washroom today, alternating between vomiting and diarrhea. My head is pounding my body is aching, and I sort of feel like I want to die.

You read this and think, "ugh! I hope you feel better!" while thinking to yourself that you will try not to stand too close to me for a few days.

I have depression and anxiety. I cannot get out of bed; everything hurts, my head is pounding, and I cannot stop crying. The idea of putting on my makeup and going to work sounds like climbing Mount Everest. I sort of feel like I want to die.

You read this and think "ugh! There she goes again. She really needs to get her shit together and toughen up. We all have issues; I don't see what the big deal is. I was up late last night, and don't want to get up for work, either," while thinking to yourself I am going to mute her texts for a few days.

In both true scenarios, I am ill. I am feeling so low and so miserable; yet in the first scenario, I am deserving of your sympathy. In the second scenario, I am a drain on your energy. In the first scenario, you are avoiding me to keep from getting yourself sick, but I will not get sicker, and will probably start feeling better in a day or two; in the second scenario, you are avoiding me to avoid the irritation of my "whining", but I will continue to get sicker.

Depression lives in a vacuum. Isolation makes it worse, and loneliness and shame are its food. When we are shocked when someone we loved has died, we feel sad; when we are shocked that someone we love has died by suicide, we feel angry. We act like this is totally unexpected, and how could we have seen it coming??

Maybe you could have checked your text messages and come by to see if I had enough tissue. Maybe you could have called to see if I needed ice cream. Maybe you could have just come and sat with me. But most of all, maybe you should have listened, and let me know that it was ok to open. Maybe you could have tried to feel more comfortable with my anxiety than you are with my vomiting.

Please stop feeling surprised that suicide is a thing. Please stop talking about this and sharing the suicide hotline only when a celebrity that you liked dies. Please be open to the dark, even if it is hard. No one WANTS to kill themselves; no one WANTS to be depressed or anxious; and sometimes, when we think you are pushing too hard and we get upset, remember you are doing the right thing. We need you during the darkest bits, even if we don't want to admit it.

IF YOU FEEL SUICIDAL OR DEPRESSED AND DO NOT FEEL LIKE YOU CAN TALK TO ANYONE ***please, please, please*** REACH OUT TO YOUR LOCAL SUICIDE PREVENTION ORGANIZATION.

*THANK YOU TO MY FAMILY AND FRIENDS WHO DRAGGED ME OUT INTO THE LIGHT WHEN I JUST DIDN'T KNOW HOW TO GET THERE MYSELF. YOU SAVED ME AND I AM ETERNALLY GRATEFUL.

A BIG OLE BOWL OF GRATITUDE

June 12, 2018

Sometimes days are great. There's no reason, they just are. I woke up, pulled together an outfit in which I felt good, got the kids fed and off to daycare, made it to work on time while listening to a fantastic blogger (Rachel Hollis) read a book that she wrote. I arrived at work on time, not as early as I would have liked, but still on time. I proceeded through a good day – accomplished work that needed doing, put out minor fires (I'm not a firefighter, but seriously, there are always fires that need putting out), shipped a parcel to my sister and my nephew, shipped something that I had sold online, dropped off charity bags, did my banking, paid my property tax (all in my 30-minute lunch break mind you! Gotta love when the lines are in my favour!), finished my workday, thinking it had been smooth sailing.

And then… just as I was heading out the door, knowing I will be able to get to the daycare on time, I was stopped by a colleague that noticed another fire smouldering in a corner… so back to booting my laptop, calling Purolator, hunting down the errant parcel, re-directing it, and closing down again… crisis averted. Until my co-worker and friend said "Kali, does your daycare charge you when you are running late?" … yep… a dollar a minute… "GO!!" she says as she shooed me out the door. I ran to my car and prayed for decent traffic.

The odds were again in my favour! It is a GREAT day. I made it to my end of town in time to pick up a plant, gas my car and *still* make it to the daycare with 5 minutes to spare. When I opened the door, my kids started going nuts that they want all you can eat tacos… it was tempting to go to a restaurant and fast food it, but given that we had just started our simplification and low waste movement *yesterday*, I figured it was a bit soon to give up and go for take-out. I offered to make tacos, to which my daughter whined "*but it won't be **all you can eat**!*" as though the idea of overconsumption of quasi-Mexican food would win me to her cause. Then my son started shouting out different restaurants, and foods, as we drove to the store. They had convinced themselves that I would give in. I did not. But I firmly, and contentedly, purchased what we were missing for a taco dinner. This had been a great day. It could only continue. Right?

Well, this is where the wheels really started to come off – my son decided he needed Gatorade. And chips. And cookies. And candy. My daughter wanted Pocky. Or maybe Oreos. Or maybe cookies? I reminded them we were just hungry, and it was dinnertime.

Back in the car, my daughter started asking to play with her friend… I reminded her that she had chores, homework, dinner, then bed. At home, my son started to climb on the remaining charity bags in my kitchen. My daughter decided it wasn't her turn to do the cat chores. My son wanted to wear a giant blanket around the kitchen, knocking things to the ground. My daughter had a million things to talk to me about, which I really loved, except for the fact that she has taken to speaking in a very silly, babyish, lisping voice that is nothing like her real voice, and it just grated on my last nerve. (I know. I am totally mom of the year…)

Amid the dinner/chore/lunch packing/chaos that is my family in the evening, my husband came home from a long day. He was tired, and sore, both from his job and from my brother's Ninja Warrior birthday on the weekend. I tried to slow down through dinner, while fielding texts from coworkers and friends, trying, albeit not very well, to remember that dinner table is family time and I am not a 15-year-old who should be texting. After dinner, I tried to remind myself that tired as I was, it had been a great day. Things had, overall, gone well. There had been no disasters. There had been no trips to the hospital. And then bedtime brought a fight. Nothing worth noting here, but let's just say it put a damper on the day, and caused everyone to be going to bed 3hrs late, me to be "putzkying" around my kitchen until 1:00AM (I am truly my mother's daughter), pitting cherries, and washing dishes. I decided to put Rachel Hollis' *Girl, Wash Your Face* back on, and while I listened to her stories of gratitude, I was compelled to blog this.

On days when things start to go badly, there is the easiness of writing the day off as a bad day. But when you sit down and take stock of your day, or your week or your month, it's just not that bad. If no one has died, and there have been no fires (like, *actual firefighter fires*), your cat is still home, you have food to feed your kids, you have friends and a job, a telepathic mommy that you can call when you feel at your wit's end, and randomly texts you at ***exactly*** the moment you needed her (or a BFF, or a sister, or a neighbour, or… you get the idea), then it's ok to let go of the not so great stuff – the whining, the fighting, the relentless demand for tacos – and think – yeah, sometimes days are just great.

IT COMES DOWN TO RESPECT

June 15, 2018

I am an introvert. I know, dear reader, that based on some of the opinions and choices that I have made, or presented, you may be feeling this cannot be the case. People tell me all the time that that cannot be, as I am loud and colourful, and sparkly, and love to laugh. But I also need my space. I need to physically remove myself from large groups of people, and after work, all I want to do is go home and lay in my bed, snuggling my kids and reading a book. I need that mental break.

I am a people pleaser. I go out of my way to say yes to everything. Go to dinner? Yes! Go to a movie? Yes! Go camping? Yes! Hang out? Yes! Babysit someone's kids? Yes! I say yes so often that sometimes I double book myself. Sometimes I agree to things with people I don't even really want to spend time with because saying no makes me feel like I am letting people down. So, I say Yes!

Now, as an introvert, all these yesses get my anxiety up and out of control. I literally cannot say yes to everything, live my life and be all things to all people. It's not doable. When I say Yes! I genuinely have every intention of following through and am excited *at the time* at the prospect of whatever I have agreed to. But then life happens, and every so often, I will get a text asking to reschedule, and it feels like the balm to my soul. People cancelled and now I have time to curl up and do my stuff, without guilt.

Now, this is the part that brings me shame – I am saying Yes! to everything so that I don't let people down, but then I overwhelm myself and I end up flaking out on people. I give up because I cannot bring myself to go out, or I have not got room in my budget for the event that I thought would be fun but forgot to budget for. This ends up being more disappointing than if I had said no in the first place.

I had a conversation with a friend at work today, and it really gave me pause. My friend is a confident, well-spoken, smart, funny, awesome woman, and she told me that she absolutely hates it when someone "bails" on her. She says she feels disrespected; and suddenly, all these years of people being annoyed with me for being late or for rescheduling, or for cancelling all together took on a different light. I always thought that as I feel relief at cancelled plans, others did, too. But I realize that maybe that isn't true. Maybe instead of giving them back the time that they would have "wasted" with me, they are feeling that I do not respect them or their time and that maybe the time with me would not feel like a waste. Maybe my siblings, friends, family, coworkers want to spend time with me.

In my attempt to please everyone, I am not pleasing anyone at all. And in cancelling, I am making my friends and family feel like they are not valued. They feel like I am not showing up for them, and there is seriously nothing in this world that would make me want to make the people I love feeling that way. So, to that end – if you have ever felt disrespected by my flakiness, please, please know that it was not meant in that way and that from now on, I will hold myself to a higher standard.

And to my friend who finally explained to me what everyone else has probably been feeling – thank you. Thank you so so so much.

END TOXIC MASCULINITY

July 29, 2018

"Men hate crying, they rarely do it. But when a man cries over you, you can be sure that he loves you more than anything..." - Anonymous

I came across this quote the other day while scrolling through the black hole that is the internet, and while I know that the person who posted it most likely saw this as a romanticized ideal of manhood, I could not hate this more if it was a picture of a snake. Or a beet. Or a snake eating a beet. Anyway, I digress...

To me, this quote is the epitome of toxic masculinity!! Why do men hate crying?? Because we teach them from a young age that "boys don't cry"; that if they cry, they are "wusses" or "pansies", or worse yet "GIRLS"!!!! If you make your partner cry, it is unlikely that you can be sure that he "loves you more than anything" – rather, like you, he is not a robot, he has feelings, he has emotions, and he has physiological reactions to his emotions, just like *gasp* dare I say it??? A HUMAN!!

Please do not attach nonsensical sentimentality to the basic human need to cry, and instead realize that THEREFORE we need feminism – we need to teach our sons that boys DO cry – they were given tear ducts, just like girls!! We need to smash the patriarchy so that when we watch grown men overcome with emotion at losing the World Cup, we don't snicker amongst ourselves and look away uncomfortably. We need to remember that if a man rarely cries, it's not because he hates doing it, it's because he has been indoctrinated to fear the repercussions of shedding tears and we need to take all steps to end this cultural bias.

"SALT IS STRANGELY SACRED"

August 17, 2018

I find myself most at peace by the sea. The ocean calms me and speaks to me in a way that no other place can. I love the vibrancy of a city, and the beauty of the forest, but I feel most centred at sea. On a beachside, with my toes buried in the sand, the wind whipping my curls, and the sound of the waves crashing against the shore, the tangy salt air, the damp freshness. This is my home. For some, the beach is a place to visit on a sunny day, and while I admit that the beach is Gloriana on in the sunshine, I am just as apt to find myself at the shore in the rain or on a gloomy day.

It is hard for me to say what it is about the Ocean that my soul connects to, but connect it does, and so I go seeking the manna that it needs. And like a miracle, I feel replenished and content.

WHY I WON'T USE THE WORD "TRIBE"

September 24, 2018

Ok, so you all know that I pray at the Church of Rachel Hollis. That woman is my aspiration. If You know me, you will have heard about her phenomenal book Girl, Wash Your Face. I sincerely feel that that book was the wake-up call that I did not even know that I needed. I love it, I love the message, and I love the community that I have discovered in my knowing her. But I will not use her word for we band of merry few. I will not say that I am a member of the Chic "Tribe". I will be a Chic Devotee, a Chic Sister, a Chic Follower, a Chic Fan, but I cannot be a Chic Tribesperson.

Why you might ask?

When the word Tribe is a current term in our lexicon for a group of mostly twenty and thirty-something white, heteronormative women? Why won't I appropriate that to refer to myself and my friends? Because of that little word right there – the 4th one into the sentence? Yeah, that one – appropriate. The word Tribe is being tossed around like it is no big deal, it's just a word, but this is not true. A Tribe is, by definition, a group of families or people with shared ideals and interests. That indicates a lack of cultural appropriation, correct? A clan is a Tribe. A group of cheerful, hustling women should also be a Tribe, right?

Not in my mind.

To me, and to many others, a Tribe is a traditional group or gathered group of First Nations belonging to the same clan, region or traditional land. In many cases, the Instagram Tribes are exclusive of the peoples for whom the word Tribe bears significance. I fully appreciate that there is no ill will intended with the cliquey, floppy hatted, distressed denim wearing influencers who refer to their following as a Tribe, just as I am sure that most people who use terms like "out your cotton-picking mind" or "gypped" do not realize the innate offensiveness of these words. That, however, does not allow space for those of us who *do* know to carry on in this manner. If you know better, you are obligated to do better.

As a woman of aboriginal heritage, who presents as a heteronormative white woman, it is incumbent upon me to make these missteps known. I do not say this to attack anyone who has used the term, as I have been guilty of such word crimes myself in the past, and I am sure to slip up again.

But not on this topic.

Not when I have the option to use so many appropriate words that do not appropriate their meaning from peoples who have been effectively colonized into nonexistence by the ancestors of these Instagram influencers.

So welcome to my village, my community, my group, my inner circle, my fam jam, but not my Tribe.

Never my Tribe.

9/11 MEMORIAL

September 28, 2018

This is a hard posting week, you guys. 17 years ago, today was my first day of classes at UBC. I had had the fun of Frosh week and was about to head to my first day of classes when my mom called me and told me to watch the news before, I went to school because she thought I should know before I got there. As I watched the first tower burning against that ridiculously blue sky, the second plane struck the second tower and my heart ended up in my throat. That was something I was unprepared to see. Something I did not know how to understand. So, I stared at the screen agape and then went to class. The campus was sombre. The professors were understanding, except for one, who opened our class with the post-apocalyptic scene from the opening of Terminator 2. It was so disturbing because for the first time in my life it felt like I was living in a terrorized film. This was my first true encounter with that level of mass violence, and it hit very, very hard.

So, I did what I always do when I am in a panic and I wrote. I wrote a letter to President Bush, to whom I had hitherto disagreed mightily, and expressed my support on behalf of Canadians, as millions of my fellow citizens rushed to the aid of our bleeding neighbour.

Today, the world is different from nearly two decades ago, and I can honestly say that I do not think it is for the good. We hate more, anger easier, and understand less than we did when were caught unawares 17 years ago. I think that the best way to remember those who were so violently and tragically murdered that day is to make their memories mean something. To do better; to end ignorance; to strive for more understanding. As for me, the numbers 9/11 will always haunt me, and I will always feel a lump of pain in my chest when I think of those who were lost.

MANDATORY REST DAY:

FIBROMYALGIA

September 30, 2018

I like to get things done. I like to try a little harder. I like to push myself a bit more. I have fibromyalgia, which means that some days I feel good and some days I feel awful. Some days I am fighting with my body and trying to pretend that the migraine pulsating behind my left eye is just a headache and eventually the coffee and ibuprofen and naproxen will beat it into submission, and I will be able to function. Some days I wake up with little to no pain and feel like I need to get as much accomplished as possible on that day because I know what is coming next.

The problem with throwing myself at things on the good days is that I am asking for a bad day to be worse and sooner than if I could manage my days to keep them all around the middle. It is something that I am working on, but it is innately against my personality – my natural state of being is to want to do 50 things at once, and to be as flipping fast as I possibly can at all of them.

Over the past few months, I have been hustling hard – at work, at home, here – trying to achieve a life of great things that I can be proud of. I have been developing content, engaging in webinars, preparing courses to interest all of you, meeting new people, working on Virtual Book Club (which is tonight, btw), volunteering with Women's March, Lean In Canada, guiding my daughter through her autoimmune attack… All the things, in addition to my regularly scheduled life, and an additional job at work. A couple of days ago my body started to warn me that it was ready to flare and that I needed to slow down. I listened, but not enough.

So, my body took over. My fibromyalgia said – nope. Stop. Sleep. So yesterday, I wound up in excruciating pain, and other than the mama things that cannot be put on hold, I crashed hard. Yesterday and today are cancelled as I let my body rejuvenate and take care of myself. Because there are only so many spoons.

LEARN TO REST

October 5, 2018

You know the time when your excitement, energy and motivation flags on a project? When that adrenaline no longer bounces you out of bed at 5 am, and you begin to question why you started this whole thing anyway. When you think that it won't make a lick of difference if I just quit on this; if I break this promise to myself; if I just quietly pretend that I wasn't really that into it, to begin with. When you just don't have the energy to think of anything insightful to say, and that it doesn't really matter because the world is going to hell in a handbasket anyway, so what difference is one little voice going to make if I stop shouting into the empty vacuum of the internet? .

This is when you rest. This is when you take the advice of the incomparable force that is Hillary Rodham Clinton, and you remember that this is tiring, this is exhausting, this means it's time to take a rest. But it's not time to quit, it's not time to give up the fight, it's time for a break. It's time to put down your sabre and to lay down for a moment. Time to unplug for a few hours, and to get the rest that you so clearly need. Plug in your phone, put on your jammies, cover your face in a clay mask, paint your nails, and drink your tea. Just rest. The world will seem a little brighter in the morning, and you will feel ready to head once more into the breach.

MY SON

October 5, 2018

Going home to this face is my favourite.

I love my kids so much, and I love that this little man is still small enough to curl up into a hug with me, to cuddle on my lap, and to not be embarrassed to hold my hand in public.

This boy is silly, sarcastic, witty, clever, funny, intelligent, sweet, kind, rough, and cuddly. He is so many things at once that I cannot peg him down as any one thing. He is the happiest boy I have ever seen, with natural sunshine that I cannot find anywhere, but he is also stubborn and angry when he suddenly gets the urge. He is my boy, my buddy, my baby. I could not love him more if I tried.

ARE WE LYING NOW?

October 10, 2018

I have decided that I will arbitrarily implement my own standard of rightness and wrongness.

Lately, we have been told that as women, we are predisposed to lying. If ever a woman dares to come forward to tell the world, or heaven forbid, a law enforcement officer, or court tribunal that she was sexually assaulted, we cry foul. We say that she is a lying whore; we say that she is a slut; we say that she was asking for it; we say that it never happened and that she is an unreliable *witness* to the crime that she was *victim* to. So, as I have heard that now is a bad time for young men and that the last millennia that have been a bad time for women has been nothing compared to the last year that men have "survived", I have decided that I will just start lying. All the time. About everything. Because, as a woman, I am determined to be a liar anyway. I might as well do it, if I am going to be accused of "probably making it up" to hurt someone else's career, then I might as well really give it my all!

Picture this – a world where women never tell the truth; a world where we make things up all the time; a world where whatever we say is probably just said to wreck some poor man's future. In this world, why bother just lying about sexual assault? That seems so small! We need to think bigger! Our lies and accusations need to be more audacious! Come on, ladies! We might as well be in for the whole thing – murder, fraud, robbery, insanity – let's do this!! Let's start with a simple example – you are walking through a grocery store, with a child, allegedly your own, but who is to say for sure? I mean, that's probably a lie that you made up to trick your man into staying with you! Anyway, you are in the grocery store with this random child, and the child picks up a candy and begins to eat it. You walk out of the store, with this sticky child and are stopped at the door by a security guard. The guard asks you if you intend to pay for the candy that is clearly in the kid's hand. You look at the child and then at the security guard and say with a smile "oh, I did!" and cheerfully continue to walk out. The guard stops you again and asks for proof of purchase, and now you look at him quizzically and say, "for what?" He gestures to the kid and the candy and says, "the candy that the child is eating".

"What candy?" you ask sweetly. The guard will be mildly astonished, as you had just said that you had paid for it, and beyond that, it is quite clear from the grubby face and hands what candy he is referring to.

"The one that you said you paid for. The one that your kid is eating."

"What are you talking about? I do not allow my children to eat candy under any circumstance." You will say this last part from your holier-than-thou high horse. Remember, in this world, where we lie all the time about everything, the truth is irrelevant. We just play through.

"Ma'am," the guard will say, "you have to pay for this candy. I cannot allow you to leave without paying for it."

"I don't want to pay for candy that I do not have."

"Your child has it. They are eating it *now!*"

"What are you talking about? What child? What candy??" You will blink repeatedly at this point.

Remember, from now on, in this world where all women capriciously lie constantly, there is no need to feel guilty about the frustration or anger that you incite in any man, such as the store security guard in this scenario. You are looking to ensure that he cannot do his job, and ideally, that he will be fired and destroy all prospects in his field. That is, after all, the end goal of all our endeavours as women.

Let's think bigger, ladies! Let's think massive!

Sexual assault is just *one* thing that we can lie and falsely accuse men about. It's so salacious and tawdry. Imagine this – you decide that you will own a company. You may have worked hard your entire life to do this, but who are we kidding? You just slept your way to the top and probably don't have any idea what you are doing. In fact, *you probably stole* your business start-up loan from one of those hard done by young white men that we have heard so much about. Now is the time to save yourself some money. When it comes to tax season, you will look over your tax documents, create random numbers, and file them with pink glittery gel ink, because face it ladies, we always want to spend extra money on those pink pens "for her", with that "pink tax" that we are always lying about. When you are told that you must legally use blue ink, make sure to argue that you absolutely did use blue ink. This tax officer is clearly lying to you. It doesn't matter that you can see the pink and glitter right in front of you. You just maintain that it *is, in fact, blue!!!* You can tell him that he is lying to make you look bad. He is trying to destroy your company. You can tell him you do not actually own a company. You can gaslight the hell out of him. I leave it to your discretion. In fact, you could even turn it into a sexist issue – why does the ink need to be blue? You are female. You love pink, *naturally*. Or, you could accuse him of stereotyping that because you are female it is *assumed* that you used a pink, glittery gel pen?? Seriously, you go ahead and play it however you like.

Just remember to ensure that you are a true member of the Lying Ladies population. As I continue down this path – creditors may complain that I am deeply in debt, as I will just tell everyone that I have paid my bills, while doing whatever else I feel like doing. My boss will ask me to complete a project and I will tell him it has been done, and gaslight him when he says that I have not.

What is a little crazy making in the grand scheme of things?

It is my nature as a woman to lie. My children's teacher will ask me to come in for an interview about why little Meghan is hitting children with chairs, and while I will reinforce strongly with Meghan that this is the right thing to do under all circumstances when the teacher asks me about it, I will lie and ask what kind of person do they take me for?? What kind of mother would encourage her daughter to engage in such malicious and intentionally destructive behaviour??

When I hit my car into my co-worker's very expensive new vehicle, I will point to the dented, scratched area and ask him if it is worth complaining about, as it could have been much worse. I could have ripped the doors off and slashed the tires, too! And besides, there's no damage to my car, so who is the insurance company going to believe? It's his word against mine, and there will be so much paperwork, and besides, I'm not the "type" of person who crashes into cars. I will carry on with my day.

Can't you just see it? And imagine, exponentially, if, in this world, it is not just you and me lying, but it is ALL women! We ALL do this ALL the TIME! Imagine how crazy men would feel.

Imagine the conversations they will have with their friends "well, it wasn't that bad. Karen only lies about not making dinner. My sister Elaine lied into a CEO position and she regularly throws crowbars at my brother-in-law when he gets home. I mean what is he going to do about it? The one time she managed to hit him, she lied so much that he wasn't even sure what they were talking about anymore."

Why stop there? We can falsely accuse young, rich, white men of robbery, assault, murder, fraud!! There are so many more interesting and punishable crimes that we can lie about!! Sexual assault is just the tip of the iceberg, and besides, the laws on that suck, so there isn't much strain on a man's future pursuits.

So, ladies, what do you say? Are you with me? We can make our false accusations and lies a true way of life. We can sincerely fool all men and destroy all potential for their future.

CHOICES

October 12, 2018

Every day I have choices: to sleep in, or wake up early, drink coffee or water, to cuddle my kids or play on my phone, to work or rest, etc. Every day I have a choice in my attitude as well – this isn't as straightforward though. I used to think that self-help and inspirational quotes were beautiful but not for me. I didn't think I could grow or achieve things. I didn't list goals or focus on dreams, or even have plans, because I didn't see any reason to. I was who and what I was and that was all there was to it.

I learned something, though – that is called depression. Not sadness, not laziness, it is a Major Depressive Episode, and it was not something that happened once, it was a chronic and reoccurring disorder that took away my ability to make choices. The medication that I take every day to keep my depression away also gives me the ability to make these choices every day. My Cymbalta has allowed me to see my future as something big and bright and bold. It is what allows me to wake up in the morning and write down my goals for the day. I am not ashamed or afraid to admit that I choose to take this medication for a mental illness that I did not choose to have, and that is twice as likely to occur in women as in men, per MDSC.

Every day I have choices: I could choose to feel ashamed and hide my mental illness, or I can choose to end the stigma around mental illness by speaking my truth and hoping that at least one person feels less alone.

JUST LOVE YOURSELF

October 13, 2018

Are you ever afraid to feel good about yourself, proud of yourself, pretty, smart, etc. for fear of being thought arrogant? Like if you have thought that you do not DESERVE to feel that way about yourself because you are "too skinny", "too fat", "too short", "too tall", etc.

You know what? Who gets to decide how you feel about yourself? Some random? A friend who is suffering her own insecurities. Your parents? Who? Who do you consider to be "the boss of you"? If the answer is "none of the above", then why do other people get to decide how you feel about yourself??

I'll tell you what, though – 9 times out of 10, no one else is thinking those things that you are afraid that they are thinking. And that one out of ten chance? Guess what? That person is a jerk! Or suffering their own insecurities and projecting, because the things that we most judge in others are the things that we think about ourselves. So, stop worrying about what anyone else thinks. Start feeling good about yourself. Start loving yourself. Don't love yourself conditionally.

Don't love yourself "when", love yourself NOW! Because who the frack cares, you guys, what ANYONE else thinks about you? Especially since far fewer people are concerned about your stuff. They are way more concerned about themselves, too.

THE 13TH DOCTOR!!!

October 14, 2018

In 2015, I decided to watch my very first episode of Doctor Who. I was on vacation just me and my kids and wanted something to watch while the kids were in bed. As a fan of Benedict Cumberbatch's Sherlock and sooooo many Sherlockians were also Whovians, I found Doctor Who, which was on Netflix at the time.

From the first time meeting The Ninth Doctor, until now, my infatuation with the zany, crazy, touching, silly, nonsensical, adventurous Gallifreyan protector of Earth has continued to grow. In 2017, it was announced that Peter Capaldi was stepping down as the Doctor, to be replaced when the showrunners changed. I was hesitant, like all Doctor Who fans are when I knew I would be approaching another regeneration. Losing the Eleventh Doctor had me in actual tears, and I never quite cottoned to Capaldi's take on the Doctor. I think it was because I had loved Matt Smith's portrayal so much, that the 12th Doctor's furrowed brow did not resonate well with me. Then Jodie Whittaker was announced, and I was beyond ecstatic for a female doctor, hereafter known as the 13th Doctor, and had enjoyed Jodie in Broadchurch. I was leery, as most of what he did on Broadchurch was cry and be angry, so I wasn't sure if she would be a departure from or continuation of the 12th.

Now that 11th Season is out in the world, I am so excited that the 13th Doctor brings back many of my favourite elements of 11 – kooky, optimistic, cheerful, and physical. I thoroughly enjoyed the monologue wink at changing completely, while remaining true to oneself. It felt very apropos.

WHY I WILL NOT ENCOURAGE "PURITY" FOR MY DAUGHTER

October 14, 2018

Purity Balls and a child pledging her virginity to her father enrages me – it is not what we should be expecting of our girls. And they do not "owe" their virginity to their fathers or their future husbands.

Before you get all angry about how I wouldn't understand, and in this day and age it never happens, understand this – I believed that withholding sex until my wedding night was a badge of honour and I wore my virginity proudly because I was told that sex before marriage was wrong.

It put a massively, ridiculous amount of pressure on me to be "good". It taught me that being "good" meant that pleasure from sexual activity was "bad". It put a huge taboo on sex and helped me to create a mindset whereby being bad meant engaging in activities that were not the domain of little girls.

Would I ask this of my daughter? Never. Nope. I am teaching her to be safe, to understand what is happening in her body, but a healthy ADULT woman includes a healthy sex life and sexual appetite.

I DRINK MY COFFEE LIKE A GILMORE

October 20, 2018

In high school, I was introduced to a free-spirited single mom and her bibliophile teenaged daughter. Lorelai and Rory Gilmore viscerally appealed to me. At the time, I could relate to a girl who didn't want to participate in school activities and would absolutely prefer to read an enormous stack of books.

When Rory and I went to University, I could completely get on board with having a tree to read under and wanting to go home to see my mom on the weekend. (We admittedly diverged around the whole yacht stealing thing…) As a mom, I relate to the whole free spirit parenting approach that Lorelai adhered to. I can relate to running late out the door in my version of cowboy boots and cut-offs under a presentable jacket, to feeling like I don't know what I am doing but my god I love my kids and I just want to do my best for them.

I can relate to her entrepreneurial aspirations of the Dragonfly Inn, of just wanting the best life for my family.

(Admittedly, we diverge in her disdain for her mother…)

FACING MY EATING DISORDER

October 21, 2018

trigger warning – anorexia nervosa, hypergymnasia

"Skinny Minnie." "Bony." "Scrawny." "Long and lanky."

When I was a child, I was naturally thin. I was a dancer, and even when I was diagnosed with Hashimoto's Hypothyroidism at 13, I was told I had all the symptoms of hypothyroidism but that I was skinny, so it couldn't be that. I hated being called skinny because I didn't want people to talk about my body. I didn't like it, and I didn't feel comfortable with it, and it annoyed me. Beyond that, though, comments from family were the only time that my weight came to my mind. I was tall, thin and pretty much always wore the same sized clothing. I developed to a ridiculous bust size as a teen, and my "girls" have stayed in the middle of the alphabet ever since.

Fast forward to 2012 – I had given birth to two kids, two years apart, and had gained weight. I had developed a "muffin top" over my jeans, but the thing that bothered me the most was that I could not push a toddler and two preschoolers around Disneyland in a stroller without being completely out of breath. I decided that I would take up running, as a friend of mine was doing it, and it seemed like an efficient way to improve my cardiovascular health. I downloaded the Couch to 5K app on my phone, dropped my daughter off at preschool, strapped my son in the stroller and started. It was hard but good. I enjoyed it after a while. In March of 2012, my beloved Grampa was diagnosed with Pancreatic Cancer, which has

one of the highest mortality rates of all cancers. I was not enjoying being a stay at home mom, because I was just not that keen to crawl through jungle gyms. I did not care about the things the other stay at home moms seemed to care about. I wasn't in a race to make sure that my kids could beat other kids at anything. I was depressed, stressed and terrified. I felt that I had no control over my life. I could not be with my Grampa as much as I wanted to be, because I had to get the kids home for nap time. My IBS and anxiety were completely out of control. So, I pushed myself harder and ran twice a day. Then I ran AND did workout videos in my living room. Then I downloaded MyFitnessPal and tracked every calorie in and every calorie out. I joined the fitness challenges. I began to lose weight. I was told that I looked so good, and I felt proud that I was shrinking back to my pre-baby size. I became obsessed with how thin I was. I didn't even really care how I looked, my goal became to shrink and shrink and disappear.

I didn't want to face my imminent loss, so I traded feelings for running, and sit-ups. Eventually, my weight loss plateaued, and I began to obsess about what I ate. I was suffering severe IBS, remember, so I tried to only eat things that wouldn't bother my gastrointestinal tract. I was suffering from gallstones and told to eat less fat until my gallbladder was removed so that I would not suffer a painful attack. I took this to the extreme – I began to live off broth, low-fat peanut butter, bananas and rice cakes. Literally. I had next to nothing else in my diet. I was light-headed, irritable, shaky, and confused most of the time. But I didn't see it this way. After therapy, and years of medication, I know that this was my way to control my panic and unhappiness. My life felt out of control, but I had absolute control over the amount that my hip bones

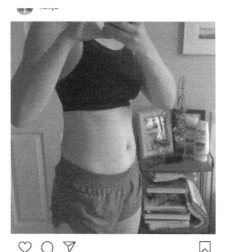

Liked by rosieandarelia and 36 others
kalijd #tmdmombody My mommy stripes - I didn't have any until the last 2 weeks of my 1st pregnancy. This body bore 2 beautiful kids and I am proud of everyone of those marks and am so lucky to be my kids' mom!

stuck out in my jeans or how deep my clavicle was. I was deep into an eating disorder that I could not admit that I had when I had a sushi dinner with my family and my brother and sister, in a rare act of solidarity, disdained my "meal" of 2 pieces of nigiri, with a huge bottle of water. They told me that I was too skinny, and why was I not eating anything. I became defensive and told them that I was full and had too many food intolerances to enjoy food. My brother asked me what I *could* eat and when I told him only rice cakes and peanut butter, they angrily told me that there was nothing in that. I was angry and panicky because I did not want to admit to anyone, let alone myself, that I was not eating anything. I did what I used to do anytime things started to stress me out – I angrily gathered my kids and said I was leaving because I wasn't going to be judged about my food.

They did not bring up my food intake after that, as we all had bigger things to worry about, as our Grampa began to lose his battle with Pancreatic Cancer, but I felt self-conscious every time I had to eat in front of my family. My family bent over backwards to accommodate my food intolerances, to reduce the stress of family meals. But I kept shrinking. After my gallbladder surgery, I lived off vegetable broth, bananas and coffee. I continued to shrink. People told me how great I looked. Except for my family. My aunt told me that I needed to stop losing weight because my cheeks were sunken. My family told me that maybe I was getting too skinny. I was offended, but as I had done nothing to handle my anxiety, stress or fear, and I still felt that my life was completely out of control, I kept losing weight. At 5'11", my lowest weight was 146 lbs, and I would justify this by saying that I

79

was at the low end of a Normal Body Mass Index spectrum, and therefore, I was fine. I was not fine. I was disappearing. I had lost my sense of self; I had lost my desire or ability to focus on reading. I spent my spare time exercising, or talking about exercising, or talking about food, or focusing on which parts of my body still required "fixing". I negatively compared myself, other people, as motivation, and positively compared myself to other people to make myself feel better. I was unhealthy. My mental health was abysmal. I was so depressed that I could not even cry. I felt numb. Then my Grampa passed away. In 2013, my heart was shattered, and I felt even more numb. I could barely function. I was tired, I could not sleep. I was hungry but would not eat. I just fell apart. In June 2013, my body took control back from me, by spinning into my ultimate diagnosis of Fibromyalgia almost a year later. As I worked on becoming healthy, I gained weight. Different medications that were attempted to figure out how to stop my pain, one of which caused me to gain 15lbs in one week. A friend of mine at the time told me that she would rather stay sick than to gain "that much weight" in one week. I felt ashamed and "fat", but as the scale crept up, and the doctors ultimately figured out what was going on, I felt happier and healthier and learned to no longer attach my sense of well being with the ability to take up as little space as possible. I am no longer "skinny Minnie" and have been referred to as a "bigger girl", but I am right back to where I was as a little girl – I don't think about my body. I am happy, and I am annoyed when people comment on my body because I am not interested in discussing it. I will not lie and tell you that I never look in the mirror and don't have a moment of pain thinking about being 65 lbs lighter, but I now I acknowledge the pain, accept that I am who I am, and know that it is more important to me to be healthy than to be "long and lanky." I am proud to use the word "fat" as a descriptor rather than as a form of self-flagellation. I am happy to see women celebrate their bodies no matter what the size, but more than anything, I am so proud to see others overcome disordered eating, and I am happy to be a recovering anorexic and hypergymnastic. I am grateful, and I refuse to shrink and disappear again.

SUUUUUUPER MARRIED

October 23, 2018

My coworkers say that Dave and I are "super married", meaning that we are as married as 2 people who have not been married for 60 years could possibly be. Last night, we put that to the test □ – I bought some hair dye at the professional beauty supply shop and asked him to read the directions and paint my hair. So, he watched a zillion YouTube Balayage and Ombré videos and then set to work. He told me that smart husbands would say no; I told him it was just hair, and I could always go back to super dark if it didn't work out.

I would like to mention that my hubby is NOT at all trained in hair styling of any kind…

Well, I guess we are "super married" because today, I am very happy with my bright, copper coloured hair, and told him so.

Is there anything that you would NEVER consider doing with your spouse? Is there something you THOUGHT you would never do and then did?

OUR INSTASTORIES DON'T TELL THE WHOLE STORY

October 27, 2018

This family was less than 3 months from the most devastating moment of their lives. The 6-week long flu would turn out to be the most traumatic, life-changing disease that our family has ever faced. The cancer was there at this point. We just didn't know it yet. My migraine went from being debilitating to pretty much the least awful disease in the room.

On Insta, we all show our highlights, our happy moments and the things that make us look good. This happy family photo is brought to you by an hour of frustration, and hour of stress and finally 30 mins of getting it together and getting out the door.

After 24 hours of a violent migraine (for me), 6 weeks of the flu (for him), 2 kids who are too excited to get ready to go, we are out the door and determined to have a fun mini break for this last weekend in October.

ROAD TRIP??

October 29, 2018

Sooooo this weekend was a freaking gong show, you guys! Shakespeare would have called it a comedy of errors, whereby nearly anything that COULD go wrong did. So, you know what? I am gonna "glad game" the hell out of it.

The drive home was spent with 3/4 of The Desautels Family reading good books, while the remaining 1/4 drove, listening to his favourite music.

We went to the very first Starbucks and it wasn't very busy, so we got to try the limited-edition Witch's Brew.

We had dinner in an Irish Pub in Post Alley, and the kids got to drink bottled root beer, which was a highlight for them.

Target had buy 2 get 1 free kids books today, and I have 2 kids, sooooo… ☐

Our hotel had cookies and hot apple cider at bedtime.

We all had a good night's sleep after watching Monster's University and a super long walk in the rain.

The kids have giggled together for 2 days straight and cuddled nicely in bed last night.

Our hotel provided a complimentary hot breakfast buffet.

And – drumroll please- we made memories that we can laugh at 25 years from now.

It's all about perspective and focus.

FALLING DOWN THE RABBIT HOLE:
CANCER ARRIVES

January 25, 2019

"Your husband has rectal cancer." The surgeon said this in the calmest, the most matter of fact way. There was nothing harsh or careless about it. Just a fact.

This must be a bizarre joke, I thought, as I quickly looked to Dave. Dave was not smiling, but rather nodding ruefully. My face arranged itself into its usual pinched expression when I do not understand something or feel leery.

"I could see it through the scope. We will need to do a colonoscopy and a CT Scan and bloodwork right away," the surgeon continued as he typed away at his computer. And armed with that information, on December 19, 2018, we held hands and fell down the rabbit hole.

In 1999, I turned 16 years old. My parents had a rule that I may not date anyone until I was 16, and that year, my friends decided to have dates to the high school Valentine's Day dance. Even my Irish Twin younger brother was roped into taking one of my girlfriends as a date. I was not keen on the idea of dating and was less than thrilled when my brother began asking his friends if one of them would be my date. My brother and I had a matching friend group – we spent our break and lunchtimes together, our friends all interacting, and hanging out, regardless of the weather, on a patch of cement outside of the Art classrooms. One morning, waiting for the bell to ring, I found myself sitting on the ground while one of his friends, a boy that I had been in split class with through most of elementary school until he began homeschooling for a couple of years until middle school. As he kicked a wet tennis ball around the cement pad, he casually said "if you can't find anyone else to take you to the dance, I guess I can", without looking at me. For years afterward, my brother would say that that was the most successful pick-up line he had ever heard. After my awkward agreement, we went to the dance, and have been together ever since. In fact, our second child, our son, was born on the 11th anniversary of that Valentine's Day dance. Over the ensuing 20 years, we have had our ups and downs, our fights and our honeymoons. In 2006, we were married; in 2008, we welcomed our daughter; in 2010, our son. We have held together, sometimes by the tips of our fingers through chronic illness, major depression, job changes, goal changes, forks in the road, and have never reached the conclusion that we would be better off apart. When asked by friends how we have "made it work", it is simply a matter of regardless how hurt or angry we are, there is no vision of our future that does not include the other one. I cannot picture myself old and grey without Dave sitting next to me, or across from me. There is no sleep in a bed alone. There is no instance where we will not come back together. There is a history, a shared life, a story of us. For the first time in 20 years, I do not know if that story will have the ending that I have so long imagined.

Over the past year, I have suggested many times that Dave should see someone. He was often tired, and his coping skills were sorely lacking. He was critical of the kids, frustrated at work, and spent a lot more time playing video games. The only times that I felt that my Dave, my best friend, the love of my life, my partner in all things, was present was after the kids had gone to bed and we were alone. Then he would laugh and smile and cuddle. Then he would tell me about his day. His go-to is to always be "fine", but I felt in my gut that he was not fine. He continued to resist, and I continued to worry and to work to keep all stresses that I could control out of his life. I didn't know what to do, and I was becoming frustrated with his lack of willingness to work to find his happiness. As if in direct opposition to this pervasive mood, I discovered Rachel Hollis and began a year of following my dreams and goals, trying to inspire him to do the same through behaviour modelling. Nothing worked. And then…

And then one day in October, I was at work, trying to beat a deadline, when he called and said "Hey sweetheart, I think that I need to see the doctor. Something's not right."

I felt both anxiety and relief – he had finally noticed that he needed help, but also – he was now scared enough to want a doctor. He told me that he had been having bloody stool since February, but that in recent weeks it had increased to the point that he was now having bloody stool roughly seven times a day. As a carpenter, and shop manager, he had been forced to stop going on installs, and to remain in the shop due to the pain and persistent pressure to use a washroom.

I made an appointment with our doctor, thinking that maybe his stress and anxiety had developed an ulcer and that we would finally get him to begin to be willing to find a solution for his moods. He asked me to join him in the doctor's office and explain what had been happening. She sent him away with myriad tests to complete and the requirement that he return within 3 weeks to discuss options and results.

Over the next three weeks, he avoided the sample kits and blood tests like the plague. My husband is extremely private and does not like to discuss bodily functions or what happens in the bathroom under any circumstance, and I thought that was the problem. Until he told me that he had not urinated in 3 days, despite drinking regular amounts of fluid. This was the day before the follow-up.

The doctor sent us immediately to the emergency room. We both left work and spent 6 hours being, what felt like, ignored by the doctor, until finally she came to us and said we could go home with a prescription for antibiotics, and rest. Dave was frustrated, hungry, tired and worried about the fact that he would not be getting paid for the missed time at work.

We went to the follow-up. Our doctor told us she would send us to a surgeon for a colonoscopy. We were given a date at the end of February, which led us to believe that the issue was not that serious. He completed the run of antibiotics and found no relief from the symptoms.

He felt worse than he had before.

Then the doctor received the stool sample results, and suddenly our appointment was the next Wednesday.

On December 19th, we would be driving to the surgeon to discuss to colonoscopy. We drove separately as I would be going to work for my annual review that afternoon, and he would be going home. The surgeon was located about an hour from our town, so we set off early.

We sat together as the doctor reviewed his symptoms and the test results. He asked us questions about family history, and past illnesses and surgeries. It was determined that overall, this was a perfectly healthy 34-year-old man, who suddenly wasn't. The doctor explained that Dave had ulcerative colitis and would need medication and regular colonoscopies for the rest of his life. He decided to perform a rectal exam in the office and a sigmoidoscopy. I left the room, because, as I mentioned, my husband is very private about this part of his life.

With sincere relief, I texted my mom and my best friend, explaining that Dave had colitis. My best friend explained how another of her close friends had this condition and that it was treatable, and that Dave would be fine. I could hear through the door as Dave and the surgeon discussed his waiting seven months to tell me that he had been having this problem. Then the door opened, and this doctor and my husband were facing me, telling me to come in and sit down. I expected that we would begin to discuss colitis, along with the colonoscopy to confirm the diagnosis.

"Sit down, please, Mrs. Desautels," said the doctor as I returned to my seat.

"Your husband has rectal cancer."

EXHAUSTION

January 26, 2019

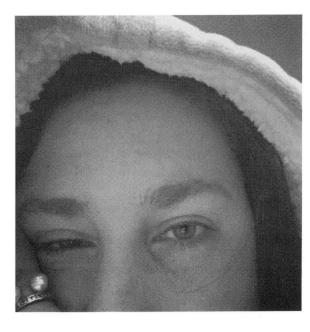

Do I look tired?

I feel tired. I feel tired all the way to my bones, and further still, if there was a further.

Today, Saturday should be a day of fun.

It should be dance class and rock wall and going out with my friends.

It should be laughter and fun and time with my husband. But it isn't and it won't be.

My husband's cancer pain is vacuous – both sucking out the air of our lives and filling the newfound space with 3AM pain, and 12am medication alerts.

The worst is still yet to come, so I feel guilty about my current exhaustion as it feels untimely and premature.

If exhaustion was an Olympic sport, maybe this would be training.

It's not though.

Exhaustion is not relieved by piling more on top.

INTRODUCING MY NEW FRIEND FEAR

January 28, 2019

Hey – have you met my new friend? This is Fear.

He's going to be shadowing me for a while. I don't really know how long he plans to hang around, but the current estimate is about 8-12 months.

Sometime last year, really in the Fall I guess, is when he decided to start hanging around, and by the middle of December, he sat me down and said that he was going to be keeping residence with me.

I've really started noticing him over the last month.

He has the funniest ways of getting my attention, including the ever-popular waking me in the middle of the night in a cold sweat. Some ways include, but are not limited to:

1. A text alert from my husband while I am work.
2. A phone call from a number I don't recognize.
3. My son's barking cough.
4. My daughter looking despondent with no reason for it.
5. My husband being unable to eat more than a couple of bites of food.
6. A deadline looming, while there are unknown doctors' appointments popping up.
7. My husband's pain painted on his face.
8. Bills that are due, while we wait for his EI Medical Leave to be approved.

This guy is socially unaware and is determined to demand attention.

Please don't concern yourself with him, and in fact, while he is shadowing me, if you could just pretend that he isn't there, that would be great.

I mean, I *know* he is there, and I *know* he is going to keep demanding my attention, but my feeling is that if I kind of treat him like a whiny toddler, and ignore his bad behaviour, maybe he will figure out societal mores and start to behave himself.

Fear is stubborn, and he might not take the hint for a while, so please consider yourself introduced and you know, feel free to talk to me but don't acknowledge or feed the fear.

IT SNOWED TODAY

February 4, 2019

It snowed today. In my part of Canada, that's rare, and I love it when the flakes begin to flurry through the air. It's a Sunday and we had nowhere to be. My kids were tired; my daughter had a cold. My husband has rarely left our bedroom in over a month, and so, we all climbed into the big bed and spent the day watching Disney and Harry Potter movies, while the snow danced outside the windows.

Sunday is not usually so quiet in our home. Our usual habit is to prepare for the week ahead, making meals, doing laundry, and getting errands done; but now, our habits are changing. When my daughter spent the drive home last night sobbing in fear, exhaustion, and the onset of a cold, I knew today would be quiet. When my son cried and feared he had been forgotten at his rock-climbing class because I was not in the building when his class ended, I knew we all needed a break.

Like the unusual snowfall, sometimes the best thing to do, to get things back to normal, is to do something different. Leaning my head back on the headboard that my husband refinished years ago before he changed careers to make working with wood his life's passion, with my small son cradled in my lap, and my pale, tired daughter holding my hand, while she snuggled against her daddy's shoulder, I knew that we were all exactly where we needed to be today.

The thing with major life events or traumas is to keep your routine as, well, ROUTINE, as possible. But it snowed today, and so we spent the day in a magical world where scary things are always defeated by love, by family, and by friends.

IN TWO MONTHS…

February 13, 2019

Two months.

A lot can happen in two months.

You could learn a new language, take up running, watch the seasons change.

Babies can be pulled to sitting in two months.

You could travel 3/4 of the way to Venus in two months.

You could heal a broken bone.

It has been two months, less a week, since my husband was diagnosed with cancer.

It has been two months since he began seeing all the doctors. It has been two months since he has begun all the tests.

And yet… he has not begun treatment. He is not perceptively closer to getting better.

In two months, his pain has gotten worse.

In two months, his anxiety level has increased.

In two months, he has been assigned to a cancer treatment team.

In two months, he has created wood burning art.

In two months, he has played all the video games.

In two months, he has become stir crazy.

In two months, he has also become an infinitely more patient parent.

In two months, he has taught our daughter to wood-burn.

In two months, he has learned to slow down and cuddle his kids.

In two months, he has remembered to kiss me regularly.

In two months, he has taught our son how to play his favourite video game.

A lot can happen in two months.

It's easy to focus on the negative. It's easy to feel frustrated and sad, but who wants easy? This is the time to learn hard things. This is the time to slow down and remember what is important. This is the time to remember the cheesiest quote I have ever heard – "today is a gift. That is why it is called the present."

Because a lot can happen in two months.

AMBER ALERT:

HOW WE LET RIYA RAJKUMAR DOWN

February 16, 2019

In 1996, 9-year-old Amber Hagerman of Arlington, Texas was kidnapped and murdered. The little girl had been riding her bike with her brother when she was grabbed. A witness told his family, and people began searching. Four days later, she was found dead less than 5 miles from where she was last seen. As of this writing, no suspect has ever been identified for her kidnap or murder.

From 1996 until 1998, people called into radio stations to alert the community that a child had been abducted. Why? Because the more people who are alerted to watch for a specific child, who has been taken, or a car, or a suspected person, the better. The more people who are looking the more chance there is of the child returning home.

In Canada, Alberta was the first to adopt a province-wide alert system for missing children in 2002. By 2005, every other province had followed suit. In 2009, Tori Stafford, also 9 years old, was abducted, raped and murdered in Woodstock, ON, and an Amber Alert was never issued as her criteria did not meet that to launch the alert. Since her case, the law in Ontario has been amended.

In recent years, Canadians had the choice to receive text alerts when an Amber Alert was issued, but in the past year, the government declared that police could simply send out an alert to cellphones when an Amber Alert happens. In 2018, **only 5 AMBER ALERTs were issued,** despite 649 missing children being reported, because the criteria for issuing an Amber Alert is so strict that 644 kids did not qualify.

644 *abducted* kids did not *qualify* as worth an Amber Alert.

644.

On February 14, 2019, 11-year-old Riya Rajkumar did not come home from a birthday visit with her dad, Rapoosh Rajkumar, and this *little girl* fit the criteria of a child for whom an Amber Alert could be issued. The Ontario Provincial Police Department issued an Amber Alert to the Peel community, to which Riya belonged, setting off cellphones across the region just after 11pm, and 911 calls began to pour in.

The Amber Alert worked.

Except it didn't.

Because these calls were not from observant people who had seen his silver Honda Civic driving by, or that they had seen Rapoosh Rajkumar at a gas station. These calls were from citizens who were angry that their sleep was disturbed over a "non-emergency" such as a little missing girl, who was soon to be found dead in her dad's basement apartment.

People called 911 to *complain* about an Amber Alert.

To *complain* that their sleep had been disturbed by a child who was abducted and murdered. To *complain* that they should only issue an alert when a child will be found *alive*.

How does this happen? How do police, who have already had to jump through hoops to confirm that a child qualifies for an Amber Alert *know* if she is alive or dead? The purpose of the Amber Alert is to hopefully find her *before* she is harmed.

I will get to my thoughts on the selfish entitlement that comes from feeling that someone else's emergency is not your problem; but first, how can anyone think that 911 is the place to call and lodge a *complaint*? How can someone, such as the caller who actually did what the Alert was meant to do and called when they saw the father's vehicle, leading to his arrest, get through to the police in time to help that child if we are using the emergency services line to lodge **complaints**?

How can we have become a society that is so ludicrously desensitized to the individual plight that we feel *offended* when an Amber Alert is issued? We update our profile pictures to be Paris Strong, or Humboldt Strong, or Boston Strong when multiple people are victims of mass casualties, and we should, but to then turn around and feel annoyance that someone's worst nightmare is an inconvenience to you? One man went so far as to post publicly that he "doesn't care that your kid is missing". Why? Why doesn't he care? We should all *care*. No, the Amber Alert does not rescue all children. No, we cannot always protect other people, but why can we not at least look at our phones at 11pm and keep our eyes open for a silver Honda with a little girl inside, who is about to end her birthday most horrifically?

Do not tell me that Canadians are kind, and welcoming and admirable and that we look out for each other while dialling 911 to tell them that *this* little girl does not *deserve* to disrupt our sleep.

In the end, despite the ridiculous selfish, bordering on sociopathic, lack of care shown by Ontarians last night, the suspect, Riya's father, was spotted by someone who understood what the Amber Alert is meant to do, and the police managed to arrest and charge him, finding Riya's body in her father's home.

The Amber Alert did what it was meant to do.

Unfortunately, humanity didn't.

CURING MY HUSBAND'S CANCER:

HOW FEMINISM CHANGED CANCER TREATMENT

February 24, 2019

Feminism is the belief in equality between sexes.

Feminism is the understanding that all people, regardless of gender, orientation, race, religious affiliation, or ability have something to contribute.

Thanks to this belief, my husband is being treated, and, if everything goes according to plan, cured of his cancer.

This week, my husband began his first week of radiation treatment, compounded with chemotherapeutic pills to aid in the destruction of the cancer cells that have invaded his body.

Every day that we have visited the radiology department, where we first met the doctor who guided us thoughtfully through the radiology department, I have whispered a prayer of thanks to Madame Marie Curie for her Nobel Prize-winning work on the discovery of radiology. I am grateful to this long-ago pioneer of women in science, and her ilk for their life-saving work.

As the laureate of two Nobel Prizes for Science and the first female Doctor of Science in Europe, Madame Curie dedicated her life to the discovery and understanding of radiation and radio particles as they pass through objects, including the human body.

Madame Curie was determined, in her lifetime, to cure cancer using radiobiology and she succeeded in the curing of surface and skin cancer lesions, before moving to the treatment of cervical cancer. Her death in 1934 was directly caused by her lifelong dedication, and thereby exposure, to the development of radiology.

The work pioneered by Madame Curie is today carried on, in my husband's case, by a Radiation Oncologist at the BC Cancer Centre, who happens to be female and Muslim.

In 1875, Jenny Kidd Trout was the first female licensed physician in Canada. An active feminist of her time (read: white Christian), Dr. Trout worked to advance the medical education of Canadian women, declaring that it was her hope that one day each large town in Ontario would eventually have at least "one good, true lady physician working…"

Dr. Trout's hope is now certainly fulfilled, with roughly 40% of all doctors, and 54% of all new, young doctors, in Canada being female, per a 2017 MacLean's article. (**https://www.macleans.ca/news/canada/female-doctors-are-on-the-rise-in-canada/**)

In this vein, our family physician is a trusted and phenomenal woman. She has been our family's practitioner for nearly a decade, and we are incredibly grateful for the pioneering efforts of women like Dr. Trout, and Dr. Emily Stowe, who advocated and opened doors for women in Canadian medicine.

In 1949, Dr. Jane Cooke Wright began work with her father Dr. Louis Wright, on the experimental chemotherapy treatments. Studying the experimental anti-cancer chemicals, and how they reacted with leukemias and lymphatic cancers, Dr. Wright advanced the treatments to the point that several of her test patients went into remission.

At 33, Dr. Wright became the Head of the Cancer Research Foundation. In 1971, Dr. Wright became the first African American Female President of the New York Cancer Society.

Her work led to the current understanding of chemotherapy, including the Capecitabine tablets that my husband is taking in conjunction with his radiation treatments, to reduce the tumour in advance of his surgery.

Today, the doctor responsible for Dave's chemotherapy, as his Medical Oncologist, is an Asian woman. The doctor walked us through the potential side effects of Capecitabine, as well as the benefits of it in conjunction with radiation protocol.

Elizabeth Gooking Greenleaf is recognized as the first female pharmacist in North America, opening her own apothecary shop, to work alongside her husband's medical practice in the Thirteen Colonies in 1727.

As no laws were prohibiting a female from practicing as an apothecary, she set up shop and paved the way for future female pharmacists. A study by Donica Janzen, BSP; Kerry Fitzpatrick, BSP…; and Linda Suveges, Ph.D., shows that females now make up more than 59% of pharmacists in Canada. (**https://www.ncbi.nlm.nih.gov/pmc/articles/PMC3676192/**)

My husband's pharmacists at the BC Cancer Centre, who spent time explaining the procedures and side effects of the Capecitabine, were both women.

In fact, the only healthcare provider on my husband's team who is not female is the surgeon who will remove the tumour. That said, when we met with him, we also met with the colorectal Fellow who is studying with him… also a female.

Feminism is the belief, or rather the *fact* that gender has no bearing on a person's abilities or skills. A team of women are saving my husband's life.

A team of women, who have followed ceiling shattering women, are saving my husband's life.

Feminism is saving my husband's life.

So, when I silently thank Marie Curie, or Dr. Jennie Trout, or Dr. Jane Wright, for making it possible for there to be the team of doctors, you had best believe that it is with sincere appreciation and ardent admiration.

MARCH IS COLORECTAL MONTH

March 17, 2019

In October, there is a blush of pretty pink objects to raise money for Breast Cancer.

In November, buildings are alight in a wash of purple for Pancreatic Cancer Month.

In March, there are ads about endangered butts in Canada. As Colorectal Cancer Awareness Month, March is ushered in with a model's bottom painted to look like an endangered species, including the polar bear. **Endangered Butts – Colorectal Cancer Canada** is meant as a light-hearted reminder of a serious subject. Using body paint, on bare bums, which are then tended and moved to animate the animal (seriously, click the link if you think it sounds crazy), providing some insight into insidious cancer.

According to the Colorectal Cancer Association of Canada (CCAC), Colorectal Cancer accounts for 13% of cancer diagnoses, second only to Lung Cancer (IN NON-GENDER DISCRIMINATING CANCERS. THE MOST COMMON CANCER IN WOMEN REMAINS BREAST CANCER, WHILST IN MEN, THE MOST COMMON CANCER IS PROSTATE CANCER) as the most common cancer in Canada.

The thing about Colorectal Cancer is that in a puritanical society such as ours, anything related to our bodily functions is a source of embarrassment. We are taught that "bathroom talk" is reserved for the bathroom or the doctor's office, thereby creating a stigma that makes talking about our rectums, or anuses, or other defecation-related subjects taboo. We blush when we pass gas, giggle when someone belches, lower our voices to mutter diarrhea, apologize for "stinking up the bathroom", and overall try to pretend that that basic human function does not exist. This means that whether we know, inherently, that we should be able to talk to our doctor's about it when we are concerned that there is a problem, we don't, because even in the privacy of our Doctor's Office, we feel the overwhelming societal humiliation deep through our pores.

So, to combat this, and remind us that giggling about our butts does not mean we should ignore them, we have **http://www.endangeredbutts.ca/**.
Endangered Butts

Since 2000, the incidence of Colorectal Cancer in younger adults (defined by the Cancer Agency as any adult under the age of 50) has increased, while Canada-wise screening has seen a DECREASE in overall instances of that cancer. So why are younger and younger people being diagnosed with a disease that is so common, but traditionally atypical in young adults? The CCAC attributes some of this to the increased rates of diabetes, obesity, lack of exercise, the consumption of red or processed meats, and smoking.

Why should you listen to the polar bear talking out of a model's butt? Because Colorectal Cancer is the second most common cause of death of males from cancer, with a 1 in 29 chance of dying from the disease. Because it accounts for 12% of all cancer deaths. Because the survival rate for adults diagnosed with any level of Colorectal Cancer is 68%. Because the symptoms are terrible. Because the longer you wait for a diagnosis, through early diagnosis, the worse the results causing more invasive and painful treatment. Because stigmas do not save lives.

Colorectal Cancer Stats

Due to the slow growth of an average Colorectal Cancer cell, it is common to be diagnosed at a later stage than some cancers. This means that you may not exhibit symptoms for months, if not years until suddenly, they arrive and quickly become unbearable. Below is the CCAC staging reference sheet:

"AFTER EACH ELEMENT HAS BEEN DETERMINED, THEY ARE COMBINED TO FORM AND OVERALL STAGE OF THE CANCER IN ROMAN NUMERALS, THE HIGHER THE NUMBER, THE MORE ADVANCED THE CANCER. THIS IS GENERALLY HOW THE CANCER IS REFERRED TO BETWEEN DOCTOR AND PATIENT:

- *0* – THE CANCER IS CONFINED TO THE INNERMOST LAYER OF THE COLON OR RECTUM. IT HAS NOT YET INVADED THE BOWEL WALL.

- *I* – THE CANCER HAS PENETRATED SEVERAL LAYERS OF THE COLON OR RECTUM WALL.

- *II* – THE CANCER HAS PENETRATED THE ENTIRE WALL OF THE COLON OR RECTUM AND MAY EXTEND INTO NEARBY TISSUE(S).

- *III* – THE CANCER HAS SPREAD TO THE LYMPH NODES.

- *IV–* THE CANCER HAS SPREAD TO DISTANT ORGANS, USUALLY THE LIVER OR LUNGS."

So, now you have seen the funny polar bear, read the scary statistics, understand the staging of cancer.

That leaves only one more thing to include in this Colorectal Cancer Awareness Month Public Service Announcement – the symptoms that should have you running, or at very least briskly walking to your doctor's office.

Common symptoms are as follows:

1. blood in your stools,
2. narrower than normal stools,
3. unexplained abdominal pain,
4. unexplained change in bowel habits,
5. unexplained anemia, or
6. unexplained weight loss.

Ok! So, **REMEMBER** that March is Colorectal Cancer Awareness. If you can #EndTheStigma for mental health, you can totally end the stigma and talk to your doctor about early detection, to hopefully nip this in the "butt" (GET IT? INSTEAD OF BUD!?!? 󠀠)

BING BONG, BING BONG!

March 29, 2019

"Who's your friend who likes to play?

Bing Bong, Bing Bong

His rocket makes you yell "Hooray!"

Bing Bong, Bing Bong

Who's the best in every way, and wants to sing this song to say

Bing Bong, Bing Bong!"

My boy has gone to Disneyland with his Auntie and Uncle this weekend to close out spring break, and my brother sent me this picture of Bing Bong on a huge pile of candy, that I can only assume is a candy store in Pixar Pier in California Adventure.

You guys, I get that Inside Out is directed at kids and that Bing Bong is an imaginary friend, but my goodness that movie gives me all the feels, Bing Bong especially. As a person who has spoken openly about mental health, I cannot stress strongly enough the importance of a movie that teaches kids that all their feelings have value and how to approach them. So, if you are not lucky enough to be running around Disneyland with heroes, like my son is this weekend, consider watching Inside Out with your kids and talking to them about the themes in the movie. It is never too early to start talking about how kids feel and why.

Also – when they talk about them, try not to dismiss them. The things that sound small to you feel awfully big for littles. And like the saying goes – if you don't listen to the small things, they won't tell you about the big ones.

Photo credit @tduperron @tidygames

KIDS CAN DO ANYTHING

March 29, 2019

Girls CAN do anything. Boys CAN do anything. Our kids have so much potential locked inside of them that it is our jobs, as parents, to allow them the freedom to explore the world, to let that potential out, whilst teaching them to be contributing members of society. It is NOT our job as parents to criticize and berate our kids so that they become people who are afraid to step one toe out of the lives that we build around them. That does not build whole, amazing people; that develops scared, anxious people who do not know whether they are ever doing things correctly.

The hardest part as parents is remembering to set safe boundaries for our kids, so that they have room to explore, without feeling it might be fun to change a lightbulb with 2 chairs stacked on top of each and a serrated knife in hand. It is so easy to fall into the trap of dictating to our kids "do this. Don't do that!" on the little, mundane nonsense like how to hold a fork. If your child is over 2, there is a good chance he can figure out how a fork works without being told over and over. Now, if he is using his fork to catapult peas across the kitchen, that might be a time to step in. We need to remember that our kids are not just OUR kids – they are whole humans with their own likes and dislikes, thoughts and goals, and personalities, and the over criticism and punishing of these little humans is akin to the joke "The Beatings Will Continue Until Morale Improves".

Give your kid space, and don't hover, and don't get after them for doing things differently than you do. If you do, you may find that your child will need A LOT of therapy, and may decide she needs to bring you to her job interviews and her first day at whatever job she manages to find that doesn't care that fully grown adult has her mom with her.

WHEN THE GOING GETS TOUGH, THE TOUGH GET HEALTHY

March 29, 2019

Wanna know what comes from a cancer diagnosis, and open-heart surgery in one family?? A reminder that our health is MORE important than the convenience of fast food. We have been working to continue to be a low waste family, and I wish that berries came in bulk ☐, but I need to protect my kids from these hereditary health concerns to the best of my ability, and that starts with modelling and providing a healthy lifestyle to them. So, I have stocked up on the necessities for the week, making sure to remember that school is back on Monday, and the kids will need their meals prepped.

Plus, how flipping pretty is a cart of colourful fruits and veggies???

BABIES 20 YEARS AGO

April 7, 2019

You have heard me speak that Dave and I have been partners for 20 years, right?

Well, a friend of ours, that we have known since we started dating came across this picture of Baby Kali and Baby Dave and sent it to me last night.

In this picture, we were in high school, he was 15 and I was 16. I was wearing my favourite highliner yellow raincoat, Dave was wearing his Umbro soccer windbreaker, and we had no idea that we would be together for the rest of our lives.

When you are in high school, you think everything will be "forever", but you have no idea what forever really means. We did not know that forever would mean bouts of depression, a baby with reflux, health issues spanning from Fibromyalgia, all the way to Stage 3 Cancer, the challenges of marriage and parenthood, many jobs, and many, many iterations of ourselves.

We did not know that we would fall many, many times, and would actively have to choose each other and to choose to love each other over and repeatedly.

It is such a good reminder of where we were 20 years ago and where we are now □

I WANT TO REMEMBER YOU CLEANING THE KALE

April 15, 2019

"I'm cleaning the kale, Mama. Why are you taking my picture? You like taking pictures of me at the silliest times, Mama."

Oh, but Little Man, one day, you will not only be too old to "clean the kale", but you will be too old to want to come to the store with me.

You might even decide you are too old to call me Mama. So, until then, I need these memories.

I need to see this picture pop up in my feed in 3 years as a memory, reminding me of that silly Sunday afternoon, when you were nine and thought the kale bunches looked like feather dusters and cleaned the kale. When you still had the softest little cheeks and outfits that you created yourself, and when you still got excited about everything.

That's why I always take pictures of you at the silliest times, because the silliest times are the memories that can disappear if we aren't careful, and I really, really want to remember this silly time.

LIFE IS A SCRIBBLY KNOT, AND IT'S OKAY.

April 24, 2019

My bestie sent me this today. I genuinely think that this is the most accurate representation of life that I have ever seen.

No matter what happens in life, there are good, calm periods, but then, suddenly everything is a mess and it seems hard to believe that it can ever get straightened out.

But it will.

The scribbly knot in the middle might be bigger some days than others, but eventually, we always find our ways out and head along towards the next scribbly knot. For some of us, seeing the end to the scribbly knot is a little harder, and we start to feel dragged down by the tangles, sometimes giving up hope altogether. If we aren't careful, the tangles can pull us so far down that we can never get back up on our own.

If you are like me and have a brain that does not always know how to keep up hope or the tenacity to get through the scribbly knot; if you are as lucky as I am to have friends and family who will grab my hand and gently pull me in the direction of the good, calm point, don't let go. No matter how hard it is, hold on to whatever lifelines that you have.

I promise the knot you are in right now WILL untangle, and then, when you get to the next one, you will have a support system and a bit more confidence in your resiliency. It's ok to be scared. It's ok to panic. It's ok to be overwhelmed. Just think of this image and remember that there is a good, calm point on the other side of that scribbly knot waiting for you.

STILL.

April 27, 2019

Still.

Lay still.

Be still.

Still breathing.

Still water.

Still your mind.

Still.

Still here.

Still night.

Still raining.

Still there.

Still young.

Still small.

Still.

Stillness.

Stay still.

Still slow.

Still of the night.

Sit still.

The air is still.

Still.

But still.

Still sleeping.

Still lovely.

Still sick.

Still sad.

Still.

Still lonely.

Better still.

Still more.

Lay still.

Be still.

Still me.

HOLY HANNAH!! HERE'S TO 10K FOLLOWERS!!!! ☐☐☐

Holy Hannah, you guys!!!

At 10:00 tonight, Ty and Danielle brought out this beautiful Butter Baked Goods cake and popped open the bubbles to celebrate 10,000 followers on Instagram!!

I am so grateful and excited, and happy, and proud, and overwhelmingly thrilled to be celebrating this milestone today!!

2 full years ago, my brother and I spoke about the goals and milestones to consider in developing KaliDesautelsReads. I had nowhere even near 1000 followers at the time, so I set myself the goal of 1000, then 2500, then 5000, with 10,000 as a crazy, way out in the distance, the white whale of a goal. I am so grateful that you all have been interested and involved and have engaged with my content and taken an interest in what I write and the books that I review and my thoughts and opinions.

As we sliced this cake, I say thank you. I look at this week and think that 2019 might just be a late bloomer and that it will turn out to be a pretty banner year for my family and friends after all. Thank you. Thank you, thank you, thank you!!

LIKE PANDORA:

WHEN I SCATTER MY FEARS LIKE ASHES

May 5, 2019

I don't know how to not be scared. I don't know how to keep my fears in a box and pretend they aren't there. Don't get me wrong – I can wrestle them into the box, and I can push the box away from myself, but, like the mythic Pandora, I am unable to stop myself from opening the box again, and "with [my] hands and scatter[ing] all these and [my] thought cause[s] sorrow and mischief…"**(Works and Days ~ Hesiod)**

I have this bipolar desire to both hide from things that scare me, and to pull my fears out, and lay them on an examining table with a microscope. I don't want to see them, I don't want to think about them, I don't want them near me; and yet… and yet I am afraid that if I don't peer into the box and poke at them, they will spill out of the box from some secret crack that I didn't know to stopper. I insistently tell myself that my fears will NOT rule my life, that I oversee my emotions and reactions; I have nothing to fear. But then the crack shows up, I will notice it out of the corner of my eye, or imagine that I do, and I will rush to pull out all the "diseases… bringing mischief" **(Cont'd Hesiod)** to my soul. I scatter them on the table and feel the tightening of my chest, the fight or flight, the desire to escape, matches by my desire to climb under my favourite heavy, green blanket and to remain there forever.

What is it about fear? What is it about its power? How can I control my life when I am constantly pulled back to my fears? How does a looming deadline, exacerbated by a cancer setback, followed quickly at the heels by my son getting hurt physically while out with his friends, and my daughter feeling hurt emotionally suddenly feel like it is all too much to bear when our Employment Insurance comes to an end, and my Caregiver Leave does not get paid? How do I teach myself to handle the stressors, without giving in to the malignancy of the fear? How do I remember that this is a season of life, and for better or for worse, it will pass? How do I find my centre, when the centre keeps moving?

"Only Hope remained there in an unbreakable home within under the rim of the great jar and did not fly out at the door; for ere that, the lid of the jar stopped her, by the will of Aegis-holding Zeus who gathers the clouds." **(Cont.' Hesiod)**

Does hope still live there, even when my fears are scattered around me like ashes? I think so. I think that hope is the only thing that stops my fears from winning and the only thing that gives me the strength to wrestle them back into the box. I think that the hope, or the belief, or the faith that things will get better.

"King Solomon once searched for a cure against depression. He assembled his wise men together. They meditated for a long time and gave him the following advice: Make yourself a ring and have thereon engraved the words 'This too will pass.' The King carried out the advice. He had the ring made and wore it constantly. Every time he felt sad and depressed, he looked at the ring, whereon his mood would change and he would feel cheerful"
-ISRAEL FOLKLORE ARCHIVE # 126 **Origin of "This, too, shall pass"**

So, like King Solomon, in the night, as my fears overtake me, I look to the dainty, delicate semicolon butterfly tattoo on the inside of my left wrist, and I remember that my fears are not new – they are different, and they are bigger, and they are volatile, but they are not new – and that I have survived before, and I will survive again. I look at the elaborate tattoo on my right hip bone and see the reasons that I must keep hope. The reasons why my fear must be wrestled back into the box again, and again; and I hope against hope that I will learn to leave the box well enough alone. That I will learn to handle my fears before they find the crack through which they might seep, and that, I will learn to be more hopeful and less fearful.

WHY WE SAY WE ARE FINE

May 11, 2019

People really, really want you to be ok.

Your friends and family want you to be happy. Your coworkers want you to be fine.

Not just in a "how's it going?" I'm fine kind of way, but in a legitimately want you to be fine kind of way. We have a habit of thinking that if we say "I'm fine" we are saying it because the other person doesn't care, but we aren't.

We are saying "I'm fine" because we aren't ok with how the questioner will react. We're not ok with the concern, or the pity, or the sadness they will exhibit if we tell them what is going on in our minds. We are not ready to see our sadness, or our fear or our anxiety reflected at us. We are not ok with crumbling.

In my day-to-day life, people ask me all day, every day how I am. I usually reply "fine, thanks and you?" Or "I'm ok! How are you?" Or "Great, thanks, and you?" Or my favourite for all moods "Awesome. How are you?" I could tell you that I reply that way because they don't care one way or the other, and in some cases, such as the cashier at the grocery store, or the guy calling to sell me toner, they are only asking as a polite way to get from Point A of their jobs to Point B of their jobs, and really don't care. I could say I was moving to Mars to marry an alien and they would likely chuckle or quizzically look at me before carrying on with the chores of their jobs.

But when someone who cares about me, who talks to me daily, who has even a moderately vested interest in my well-being asks how I am, and I reply with any of the above, it is foolish and reckless to say that I am saying that because they don't care about the "real" answer. To say that takes away the human connection that we have in our lives. To say that is a nasty, easy, awful way to allow ourselves to sink deeper into the sad, fearful, awful feeling that we are avoiding.

I say this from experience. I say this from both the depressed, sad, anxious woman who took away the agency of my friends and family by bitterly thinking that they only wanted to hear that I was fine; and I say this from the sad, scared, stressed-out woman that has too many plates in the air and a strong conviction that if I drop one, all the other ones spinning above my head will come crashing down to my feet.

In the first instance, I told myself that people do not care if I am fine or not and that they only want to hear that I am fine, so they can carry on with their day. This, my friends, is BS. This is the thought of a depressed, isolated, unhappy person who does not know how to move through the fog that has darkly clouded over her brain. This is the thought of someone bitterly, mentally, and emotionally lashing out, even in her own head. Worse still, it is not giving the asker the courtesy of correcting the supposed lack of care that I am imposing upon them. I have given the asker a role, and determinedly, doggedly, angrily refuse to recast them.

n the second case, the position that I find myself in right now, I cannot bring myself to look the asker in the eye and say "I'm hurting. I'm in pain. I'm scared. I'm overwhelmed. I'm terrified. I feel like my life is falling apart, and I don't have enough sandbags to keep it from breaking."

I do not want to say these things because I will cry. I am not ready to drop my aerial plate show. I need to make it through one more minute, one more hour, one more chore before I can sit down and allow myself to feel these things. I am not saying I am fine because you don't care, I am saying that I am fine because I know that you do. I am desperately hoping that if I can keep saying that I am fine, I can be strong, and brave and that I will make it through one more day without the levee fatally cracking. I know that when you ask how I am, and I say that I am fine, you really want me to look you in the eyes and you want to say "no, you're not. Of course, you're not, and I am here for you."

I know that is what my friends and family and coworkers and acquaintances, and so on and so forth are thinking. I know that you *do* genuinely care. I know that you want me to tell you the truth. I know that I am not saying that I am fine for your benefit; I am saying it for mine, because I have a job, and kids, and friends, and family, and I do not want to say I'm not. It's so much easier to keep going if I am fine. It's so much easier to not have the stressors that are trying to break me succeed if I am fine; because right now, my "I'm fine" is the mental equivalent to Atlas holding up the world. My "I'm fine" is keeping things in their place. And if I tell you the truth, it would be as if Atlas shrugged.

So please know that when someone asks you how you are doing and you say fine, you are not saying that you are fine for them, you are saying it for you.

SHE GREW UP TOO FAST

May 18, 2019

Last night was opening night for my daughter's play, and as I watched her sing and dance and walk around the stage in a myriad of costumes, I kept thinking that's it was incredible that that young lady was my baby girl. She is tall, and grown up, and animated, and dramatic, and beautiful. Since she was born, I have been told to "enjoy these years because they go by so fast" and I genuinely believed that I was doing my best to enjoy the years between all the daily messes of young motherhood, but as I watched her up there, it made me wish I could go back and start again, knowing that it's ok for kids to throw temper tantrums, it's ok for kids to wake you up in the middle of the night. It's ok for kids to whine and demand that you stop doing whatever you are doing and play with them. I want to go back with all the knowledge and parental wisdom that I "knew" then, but didn't comprehend, and to start over and really, really, REALLY enjoy those years. My baby girl is closer to graduating high school than she is to be a baby. My baby girl is not a baby anymore, and as much as I know I was there, I still feel like I missed it. So, new mamas, when you think we are crazy for telling you to enjoy the years of exhaustion, and diapers, and tantrums, and spilled spaghetti, and biting, and worrying that your "parenting style" is not the right one, or wishing that you had invested in the fancier stroller (stroller envy is real, my friends!!), just bear with us. It's not condescension, it's a genuine wistfulness. One day you will watch your 11.5-year-old child do something that they enjoy, and you will see them tower in height, or bravery, or maturity, and you will realize that we were right. The years went by so fast, and now your baby doesn't need you to pick them up, your baby is a young woman/man/nonspecific and you will feel just like I do this morning.

TODAY, I ACCEPT THAT MY MENTAL HEALTH DOESN'T LIKE BEING IGNORED.

May 24, 2019

Today, I started fresh. I faced my fears. I had a difficult conversation. I didn't cry 90% of the day. I sent doughnuts to the Fair Unknown because she passed her Comp Exams. I went for a walk with my confidante. I brought home roses for my grandmother. I stuck to my vegan meal plan. I painted my nails. I put eyeliner on. I did my journal.

I took 500000 deep breaths. I was given a love note from my work bestie. I listened to my Rachel Hollis incentivized Attitude Adjustment Playlist. I listened to a book called A Feast of Science.

I hugged and kissed my kids. I hugged and kissed my husband. I told my grandmother that I can never thank her enough for what she has been doing for me. I drank enough water. I checked in with my friend about a job interview. I was checked on by my friends who were worried about my mental health breakdown yesterday.

I explained my adoration of Brené Brown. I watched horses eat their hay. I walked up Mt Everest. I began my period – explaining my PMDD uncontrollable crying day yesterday.

As a friend reminded me years ago, with a sign that still hangs in my home – not all days are good, but it is good every day.

And with that, I express my gratitude and curl up for a long night's rest, medically assisted by zopiclone. And if you tsk my occasional use of prescribed drugs to help me function in a way that makes sense to me, I welcome you to revisit it my bio, where you will find that "mental health advocate" is right the list.

So here I am, normalizing medications used predominantly by those who suffer from mental health concerns.

WAITING IN THE WINGS

June 3, 2019

My girl is finished her second year of musical theatre. I have watched her throw her whole heart into James and the Giant Peach, learning the lines and lyrics to every single part including her own. I have watched her battle her reticence to speak up, her anxiety, her personal challenges, and develop her confidence on and off stage. I have watched as she let her inner comedienne loose and laughed and found joy in her expressive character. Today, I got to stand with her in the wings as she prepared for her final performance of the year.

My sweet girl, taller than the others, but still my little one, standing slightly closer than usual, but not quite reaching for my hand; I know that she was happy I was there, but also strong enough in that moment to not need me to physically hold her.

This is being her mom. This is my girl; from the moment she was born. This is the kid who made me a mom. This is the kid of my dreams, better than I ever imagined, filling me with pride and love. This is my girl, right before her very last dance of the year, before she strode confidently onto the stage, and out of her comfort zone.

"DO ALL THINGS WITH LOVE"

June 8, 2019

Do all things with love. What does that mean to you? Love for yourself? Love to your family? Love to your friends? Love for humanity? Love for your job? Love for Mother Earth? Love for your God? Love for animals?

For me it means all of those:

- love myself = mental, spiritual, and physical health

- love, my family = walking alongside each one as much as possible, helping where I can, listening where I can, or sending incessant gifs wherever (in)appropriate

- love my friends = listening to them, helping where I can, genuinely caring for them, thoughtful gifts (I was raised with "little I love you's" and giving is one of my love languages)

- love for humanity = do all things with kindness, speak for those who cannot, and in essence – do unto others, as you would have them do unto you. Or as Michelle Obama says, "when they go low, we go high". Respect the cultures, beliefs, and pain suffered by others, and learn from it. Learn it well and without defensiveness.

- love my job = do my tasks to the best of my ability, be available, and genuinely, truly care about the outcome of my tasks. Respect the organization by sharing our good works whenever possible, and striving to bring success to my team

- love for Mother Earth = lowering my carbon footprint, teaching my children and modelling low waste behaviours, making small changes every day to respect her, and take moments every day to appreciate her in all her beauty, in all her turmoil, in all her spirit

- love my God = remaining connected to my spiritual, optimistic, and ritualistic beliefs.

- love for animals = creating an environment where they are safe and loved. Space where they are not harmed for frivolity. This one has taken me the longest to achieve. I spent most of my life ranging from fearful of to ambivalent to animals. It is only with the adoption and eventual mutual love for my ragamuffin Timon that I have learned to appreciate and find beauty in most animals (and through Rhe Rhe. She is seriously persuasive!!!)

« *Do everything in love* » ~ First Corinthians 16:14

I AM UNHAPPY

June 30, 2019

I have never been this unhappy in my entire life. I have been more depressed. I have been sicker. I have been more anxious. I have felt like a bigger failure. I have never been this unhappy.

When I am in the throes of a major depressive episode, I think "I am so tired. Life sucks and then you die." When I am so sick that I can barely move, I think "I feel so horrible, I think I am going to die." When I am suffering an anxiety attack, I think "oh my god, I am going to die." When I feel like a failure, I think "well, I might as well be dead, since I have nothing to offer the world." (You'll notice that no matter which level of the spectrum I am at, I am dramatic, and death factors in.)

Right now, I don't feel like the whole world is awful. I know that I am doing my best. I know that I have multiple genuine causes for anxiety. I know that stress makes the body feel sick and weak. I know that there are good things in this world and in life. I feel unending gratitude, which is a significant departure from the numbness and void of depression. I see beauty in nature. I smile at babies. I cuddle with my kids. I laugh with my friends. But I am desperately, hopelessly, despairingly unhappy.

I am unhappy because I do not know what is going to happen. I feel a complete lack of control in my life. I am unhappy because I am scared. I do not know if my family will be stronger or crumble under the weight of 2019. I am unhappy because my kids are scared and unhappy. I am unhappy because I am overwhelmed. I am unhappy because I do not know how I will manage. I am unhappy because my husband is undergoing major surgery in less than a week. I am unhappy because no matter how much I prepare; I will never be ready. I am unhappy because there is an expectation that I should not be. There is an expectation that I should be fine with my partner of more than 20 years having this surgery because he will be "fine". I am unhappy because he is undergoing surgery that has only been done 1000 times in Canada, and they are not sure about the long-term likelihood of cancer reoccurring.

I am tired of being told everything will be fine because even if it *will* be fine, it's not right now; and as much as I want to remain positive, I need to be mindful of our present moment, and this moment sucks. I am unhappy and I need to be allowed to be unhappy. I am hopeful, and thinking positive things, and feel gratitude, and am trying to establish boundaries, and say no, and not take on more than I can handle, and all the things that I am *supposed* to do in my present situation. But it still sucks. And I am still more unhappy than I have ever been in my life.

HAPPY CANADA DAY 2019

July 1, 2019

Today is an interesting paradox – I love my country, and am proud to be a Canadian, glad to have the privilege of birthplace; while at the same time, the celebration of Canada Day is the whitewashing of my First Nations ancestry – we act as though Canada was born in on July 1st, 1867, but that indicates that we weren't here before that day.

In truth, First Nations people, including my ancestors who would eventually be relegated to the status of non-white AND non-aboriginal Métis, were here for millennia BEFORE 1867.

So, as you proudly wear your red and white, and eat your hot dogs, and drink your beer, and enjoy not having to work on a Monday, please remember that our history stems back thousands of years before colonization and that if you are truly celebrating Canada today, you are celebrating ALL parts of Canada, not just the forming of a white nation imposing its values on ancient people's.

HOSPITAL UPDATE

July 7, 2019

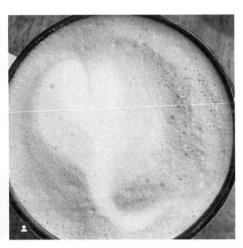

Dave came through the surgery fine. He has received the ileostomy (reversible) instead of the colostomy (permanent). We have not yet seen his surgeon and won't until at least tomorrow.

He is resting, but quite uncomfortable. He cannot have visitors for a little while yet, at least until they can get his pain under control.

That said – he is being a trooper and taking an active role in his own recovery, doing everything recommended by the nurses and doctors to help himself move through the recovery as quickly as possible.

Thank you all so much for your messages and prayers and vibes and energy. We are so grateful to have you. I am sorry if I have not replied individually to a message and will be replying over the next days as he improves, too!

We appreciate that many of you would like to see him, but for now, the doctors want him to rest and work through his pain as much as possible.

Love Kali

THIS ROOM

July 10, 2019

It is noisy in this room, but you have found peace in sleep. The bustling Bulgarian family on the other side of the curtain; the shuffling and snoring of the other men in the room; the busy swish of the nurses as they check vital signs and answer pleas for relief all over the unit. Quiet is hard to find. You escape to your dreams, which are just as noisy and vivid as this room, but you have found peace, for a moment at least.

Your body was cleaved, and the unwelcome invader was evicted, squatters' rights revoked. The tubes issue fluids which are meant to keep your battered body in comfort and help to return it to good health. I am sitting next to you, fanning your hot face, and warming your cold feet and hands, waiting for you to need a sip of water, a cool cloth, or a fresh sheet.

There is a helplessness that floats in the air in the curtained privacy of your bed. I can do nothing to heal you, you can do little to push back against the pain. You will never realize how many people have offered you and I help and comfort, but at this moment, in this room, you don't want anyone to see you like this, and we have created a microcosm of our world. It's crazy that the world is going on outside while we sit in semi-darkness, listening to your hiccupping neighbour and the gentle rattling of your IV machine.

The thing that makes me feel better about this little, noisy, dim room is the idea that cancer will be left here, in the hospital, and in a few days, we will go home, and find ourselves once again in our own quiet room.

THE ANNIVERSARY OF THE DAY THAT THE SH*T HITTETH THE FAN...ETH

July 11, 2019

Today is a weird anniversary for me – 5 years ago today is what I fondly think of as the "Day the Shit Hit the Fan". 5 years ago, today, my body started to fight me again for the first time in 10 years, my anxiety and depression became completely unmanageable, and I spiralled into a months-long search for answers to help me get out of bed and back into my life.

I remember needing to sit down at the butterfly release, and then I drove my son to an ultrasound and I could not get out of the car, because I was shaking so badly and all I wanted to do was climb out of my own skin. When I got home, I laid down and could feel the bed vibrating from my own shaking form.

5 years ago, today, the grief of losing my Grampa, my eating disorder and over exercising triggered my autoimmune thyroid disease to change drastically, and I began the long journey to my eventual fibromyalgia diagnosis.

That was a hard, hard year. At the time, it was the hardest year of my life. My ability to parent my kids suffered, my ability to function as a person and a wife and a friend not only suffered but completely fell apart. I did not know that this beating of my soul would result in the largest amount of growth that I had had in decades. When I became well, I could not imagine how happy and healthy I would feel. I could not imagine how much love I would feel for others, nor how much confidence I would find. I also had no idea that this anniversary would find me in another hospital, working through an even more insane year of "growth".

All I can hope is that 5 years from now, this will feel like a long time ago, too, and that the changes will be just as meaningful as the ones leading to the anniversary.

THANKS, MOMMY

July 13, 2019

This has been a long week, and without my mom, I am not entirely convinced I could have managed. From moral support to hotel extensions, to a walking companion, and personal food bringer, my mom has gone above and beyond. I am so grateful for the love, attention, and generosity this past week, and every week, of this woman.

PUPPY KISSES

July 28, 2019

I used to fear dogs. And night. And long car rides. And other people.

And all that that did was make my life small and make me miss out on the good things in life.

My anxiety held onto my life a fist, and it decided what I did or didn't do, and what I enjoyed and didn't enjoy. I feared dogs barking, licking me, coming near me, jumping on me… I was pretty much afraid of everything all the time.

So how is it that the best part of my day for this weekend has been laying on my brother and sister (in-law's) living room floor petting and being licked by an affectionate beagle who likes to talk? Because my family and friends took the time to talk to me about how my anxiety was ruling my life. They took the time to encourage me to get help, and 5 years ago I went onto Cymbalta and amitriptyline for my fibromyalgia which had the "side effect" of also managing my anxiety and elevating my mood.

As everything that has happened this year happens, I can't help feeling grateful for the people who have made it possible for me to get to the doctor and rebuild a life that includes the good things in life, like puppy kisses, and long drives in the mountains.

CANCER-FREE CAKE

August 10, 2019

Happy First Day of the Rest of Our Lives! Yesterday, we received the mind-bending amazing news that Dave is in remission from Stage Three Colorectal Cancer. Our daughter made a celebratory "F*ck Cancer" cake, and we shared the news far and wide. I have literally not felt this happy since well before we finally had a diagnosis for his health troubles in December 2018.

There will be no more treatment. No more chemo. We are now in the recovery phase. The recovery and monitor phase where we can see how he does over the next three months. The phase where we focus our attention on the ileostomy and life with an ostomy pouch. I have both of my kids with me – albeit hanging out with their friends. My husband is working on his wood-burning, for energy he can expend, and I feel at peace.

I hope you all have a relaxing weekend! I hope that whatever pain you are going through will resolve itself in a way that also brings you peace.

CARING IS COOL

August 15, 2019

Can I just talk for a minute about caring? I have been told my whole life that I care too much, that I need care less, why do I care, etc. The thing is that there is a difference between caring and pleasing. What I do too much is trying to please others, what no one can do enough is care. I feel like I need to care because if no one cares, who takes responsibility for things? It's ok to care about politics, and civil rights, and your family, and your job, and your car, and your garden, and your kids, and animals, and the planet, and how you affect each of these. In fact, it's not just ok, but it is highly, highly recommended.

So, take care, show you care, be caring, be careful. Care about the turtles and the pangolins; care about the ozone layer and the political effects on climate change; care about the old man who lives on the corner and the homeless woman who rummages through your recycling for cans and bottles. Just care. It's easy to be a misanthrope, but being a caring person? That's the hard part, but it's worth it.

Just give it a try.

13 YEARS OF MARRIAGE

September 16, 2019

13 years ago, today Baby Kali and Baby Dave married. We had no idea what being married was about, other than we got to be together all the time, live in our own house, and eventually have kids. We did not think about job changes, and health challenges, and the fact that our kids would have minds of their own. We just figured we would be married, and everything would be great.

And for the most part, that's true. If there is anything that this past year has taught us, is that even when we are annoyed with each other, or in the depths of pain, or angry, or scared, or, or, or, there is no one we want beside us more than each other. His smile, when his dimples show and his blue and brown eye sparkle, his laugh, his passion for his work, his ability to make the kids squeal with laughter, his desire to always keep learning, his arms around me when I am sad, a kiss on my forehead tickled by his beard, his insistence that soccer is football, his obsessive need to have everything lined up and sorted, his willingness to paint our front door red, our kitchen purple, and our backdoor teal because it will make me smile, the fact that he always smells like cedar and Douglas fir (and therefore Christmas), his attention to detail, and the way he listens to me chattering without judging, our inane conversations are entirely spoken in Monty Python quotes, and his desire to always be honourable – those are the things we did not know. Those are the things that make our marriage, and that 13 years after this picture was taken, we still actively choose every day to be in this marriage together.

ORANGE SHIRT DAY

September 30, 2019

It is Orange Shirt Day and we are proud to represent our ancestors who suffered the indignities of residential schools. « Orange Shirt Day began in 2013 as a result of residential school survivor Phyllis Jack Webstad discussing her experience when she arrived at a residential school. Webstad shared her story at a legacy of the St. Joseph Mission (SJM) residential school commemoration event held in Williams Lake, British Columbia, Canada, in the spring of 2013.[1] On her first day at residential school, Phyllis had her new orange shirt taken away from her. Phyllis' experience is used today to teach students about residential schools and their assimilation practices.

The date of September 30 was chosen for the annual event because it is the time of year in which Indigenous children were historically taken from their homes to residential schools. The event is like "Pink Shirt Day" which is an annual anti-bullying day which many school groups participate in. [2]

In addition to simply wearing an orange shirt on September 30, this annual event encourages Canadians to learn about the history of residential schools. Many communities have held memorial walks, film screenings, and public lectures to raise awareness about Indigenous history.[3] Additionally, school boards across Canada have begun to use this event to teach children about residential schools.[4]

In 2017 Jane Philpott, Canada's Minister of Indigenous Services, and Carolyn Bennett, Indigenous Relations and Northern Affairs Minister, encouraged people across Canada to participate in this commemorative and educational event.[5]

In 2018, the Department of Canadian Heritage and Multiculturalism announced it was considering making a statutory holiday to honour the legacy of residential schools, and September 30 was one of the dates being considered.[6] The Heritage Committee chose Orange Shirt Day, and it was submitted by Georgina Jolibois as a private member's bill to the House of Commons, where it passed on March 21, 2019; however, the bill failed to pass the Senate before the next election was called.[7][8] »

WANDERLUST WHISTLER

January 23, 2020

"Feet, what do I need you for when I have wings to fly?" ~ Frida Kahlo

My heart is singing with gratitude to the @wanderlust fest team for granting me a scholarship. This weekend was abundantly, immensely, profoundly, mightily, extensively good for my soul. Breathing fresh mountain air, receiving love, energy, peace, and grounding, interacting with generous souls, and laughing with my friend, has given me the ability to rejoin my day to day life with a full heart, and greater patience.

I can't look back at any part of Wanderlust Whistler 2019 without the fullness of gratitude and joy.

I cannot ever fully express what this festival meant to me, and did for my soul, but I will try. This week watch for a full review of the weekend on my blog (link in bio), as I try to verbalize the amazing event that is Wanderlust Whistler.

SUP YOGA

January 23, 2020

What do you see here? A bunch of people trying out SUP Yoga? Some succeeding better than others, some Zen and some trying not to fall in? This is exactly that, but it is also me jumping so far out of my comfort zone, that I left it on the shore behind me.

I have never been on a stand-up paddleboard in my life. I am still in the nascence of redeveloping my yogic strength and balance, so the idea of attempting a teddy bear stand, or wheel pose on a rocking inflatable board over cold mountain water was terrifying. Which meant stiffening and over correcting my balance and posture, but in the end, I did not fall in. I stayed on my board, I breathed fresh air, and floated on the water that was still (less the rocking caused by me and the other SUP Yogis) and am proud of myself for trying something new. I think before I try this again, I will practice being on a SUP and get the feel for it.

But hey – at least I want to try it again! □

I SMELL SNOW

January 24, 2020

It doesn't snow in Vancouver very often, but when it does, it is magical. The blanket of white; the sparkling flakes; the silence; the rosy cheeks. When I was little, my parents would wake me up in the middle of the night when it would snow, so that I wouldn't miss the magic, just in case, it turned to rain before I woke up. My dad outside in his housecoat and dress shoes, gathering a snowball to bring into me in the dark is still one of my most favourite memories. This year, when my girl ran outside when we noticed the snowfall, I tried to resist the pull of the snow, and to be the responsible adult, preparing meals for while my husband was in the hospital. But after my daughter said, "come play with me, Mama!" For the second time, I thought of those nights from my childhood, and I realized that I do not want to be the parent who avoided magic with her daughter. I know that the night we spent in the yard with the snow will stay with her a lot longer than one more night of mommy making dinners.

Don't miss out on the magical moments. There are only so many of them when your kids are young.

NEVER MISTAKE KINDNESS FOR WEAKNESS

January 24, 2020

You know how people think that cats are smarter than dogs? Because cats are so standoffish, and dogs are so affectionate? According to recent studies, dogs have more than double the cerebral cortexes than cats, indicating that dogs could be twice as smart as cats. So why do we assume cats are smarter?

Because we put a premium on being "cool". We think that if someone behaves coolly towards others, they are more intelligent or stronger, so we tend to assume that when someone is kind, they are a pushover.

I posit that this is not the case. Think about when someone hurts you – anger is the quickest, easiest, and first reaction. It takes effort to calm yourself down and to put on a kind face and to speak kindly. If someone is kind to you, remember that they don't have to be. They are CHOOSING kindness every day. If they are kind to you, they are a lot stronger than you give them credit for. Anger is easy. Anger is weakness. Kindness takes effort.

Further to this – if someone shows you seemingly endless kindness, remember that NOTHING is endless, and if you push hard enough, the strongest person will snap and their ability to provide you with kindness will end. You will find that they will turn their attention to someone who appreciates their efforts and who has the strength to provide them with reciprocal kindness.

Take a minute to appreciate those who have the strength to be kind. Thank them. Show them kindness. Real, authentic kindness. In this life of Instagram posts and Facebook shout outs, it is easy to assume that posting something online counts as demonstrating how much we care about someone, but it isn't it. We all know that. If you post a picture of someone who loves you, talk about how much you love them, but then do not behave that way at home, you are not being strong. Don't take the easy way out. Choose to be strong. Choose kindness.

SPOON THEORY

January 28, 2020

I am all about the sassy, funny, silly, snarky mugs. I love deciding what mood I'm in when I make a coffee or tea, but sometimes it's about what mood I WISH I was in. When I feel worn out, sometimes a mug reminding me to smile or be happy or do my best is exactly what I need to give myself a bit of a boost.

Other times, like today, they kind of annoy me – like You Did Not Wake Up to Be Mediocre. Today, I felt like telling my mug "maybe I damn all DID wake up to be mediocre today! You don't know me, mug. Back off." Is that perhaps an extreme reaction? Possibly. Did it make me feel better? Abso-flipping-lutely.

In the Spoonie community, we work to be as productive as possible, with our limited energy (spoons), so if today you feel like you did wake up to be mediocre, or you feel like A is for Asleep, own that. You do not have to strive every minute of every day. Sometimes you can push yourself, and sometimes you can push the covers back and crawl back into bed. It's balance.

Actually? No, it's not. I'm beginning to think balance is another load of BS that we are fed to think if we just figured out an ideal formula we would all be superheroes and would fit all the 96 million things we have to do in a day into one 24 hour period. I do not think there is a magic equation. I don't really think there is such a thing as balance. Just people doing their best, or 50% of their best depending on the day. To do all the things, we prioritize, and when we prioritize, something must fall away. So, use the spoons you have, be awesome, or mediocre, and feel ok about what you need.

steps down from soapbox

BELL LET'S TALK 2020

January 29, 2020

Again – Baby Kali had no idea. The mention of Coronavirus was before the pandemic that saw Canadians enter a quarantine that is ongoing to this day. This doesn't take away from what I wrote in January regarding mental health, but it certainly changes the impact. At that point the pandemic was imminent. Now we are hostage to it. There is still no vaccine or known treatment for those critically effected by COVID-19. This was post was even before the term COVID-19 existing.

Today is one of my favourite days to celebrate – #bellletstalk day. A day when people do not feel ashamed to talk about mental illness, and a day when you can raise money for mental wellness simply by using social media or texting as you normally would.

In any given year, 1 in 5 Canadians will suffer a mental health crisis, with approximately 8% of the adult population suffering from a depressive episode. 24% of deaths amongst young Canadians are by suicide.

What does this mean? It means that while we are all worrying about the 3 known cases of coronavirus presently affecting Canadians, and taking measures to protect ourselves and our loved ones against this, there is a 50% chance that the adult sitting next to you right now is living with a mental illness. That is correct – by the age of 40, 50% of Canadians will be diagnosed with a mental illness. By bringing it out into the light, where it can be seen, the shame of mental illness withers and dies; by letting those suffering in the dark, THEY may wither and die.

Mental illness is not a personal failure. Just because something occurs "in your head" doesn't mean it isn't real. Think about it – ALL pain is in our heads – our nerve centres and pain receptors are in our brains, which is also where depression, bipolar, anxiety, and myriad other diseases live. So be gentle. Be gentle with your friends and family and coworkers; most of all – be gentle with yourself. You really are doing the best you can.

TODAY.

January 31, 2020

Today, I cried. I cried yesterday. I cried the day before that. In the past week, I have cried at least once a day. No reasons, just mid-thought, mid-text, mid-song, mid-sentence my eyes prickle, as the tears form, my throat thickens and feels tight, and I cry.

Today, I was tired. I was tired yesterday. I was tired the day before that. In the past week, I have been tired most of the day. Bone tired. Brain burning, exhausted, sleep on the train tired.

Today, I had a headache. I had a headache yesterday. I had a headache the day before that. In the past week, I have had a headache nearly every day. An ice pick through my eye, neck tightening, pulsing headache.

No. No. No, there is nothing wrong. Things are getting better. My husband is healing. My kids are happier. I work for a non-profit doing good work, with a team of bright, brilliant women across the country. I have not been hiding in my bed. I went dancing with my friends. I went to a meditative sound bath with another friend. I have done yoga. I have spent time with my kids. I have eaten healthful foods. I have gone for walks. I have prayed. I have journaled. I have worked. I have read. I have taken my meds. I have done all the things that a person is supposed to do to stave off depression.

And yet. And yet, today I cried. Today, I was tired. Today, I had a headache. Today, I am listening to sad songs and cannot sleep. Today, I feel exhausted to the very marrow of my body. My medications are doing their jobs, but I am depressed. My antidepressant is no match for the soul-searing hole that is depression. My antidepressant keeps me from dying in that hole, but it cannot keep me out. This depression feels familiar. It is not by any means welcome, but it is familiar. It slipped through the door that was left open when the grief came in.

My grief showed up unannounced last weekend. It knocked and without thinking, I let it in. Last weekend, I recognized that grief needed to come in for me to heal. To heal from a year of pain and fear. To heal from so many losses. To heal from the relief that I did not lose my best friend in the process. To rebuild a new, stronger life. As I sat with my friends, the tears began to burn and I escaped to the bathroom, recognizing that grief and depression had both made their presence known. After making my goodbyes, I sat in my car and sobbed. I sobbed and I sobbed until I did not think I could sob anymore.

The headache crept in after the sobbing, making the most of the opportunity to burrow into my brain. The headache allowed grief and depression to take the foreground, while it sat back and created a visual of an ice pick stabbed through my left temple as a means of relieving the pressure.

The headache. The grief. The depression. Fatigue. I know them all, and though I do not love them, I am too tired to fight them. I will sit with them, and I will accept them for a while, because what else can I do? Fighting them off will not send them away. Fighting them off will cause more tears. Fighting them off will cause more frustration. Fighting them off will not keep them at bay, it will just reinforce the false narrative in my head that I should feel ashamed and I should keep holding myself together. I can't. I can't hold myself together anymore right now.

So today, I cried. Today, I was tired. Today, I had a headache. Today, I listened to sad country songs. Today, I acknowledged that I will be bringing grief and depression around with me for a while. Today, I told myself to be kind to myself. Today, I decided to do my best and to forgive myself when my best is not the best. Today, I recognized that I will continue to take my meds, and go to yoga, and talk to my friends, and call my mom, and hug my kids, and feel grateful for my husband's returning health. Today, I accepted that even with all these interventions, I am depressed, I am grieving, and I am not ok. Today, I accepted that while I am not ok right now, I will be.

I will be. But not today.

NOT A POET...

February 11, 2020

Some days I write and know just what I want to say; other days I want to write but have no idea what to say. There is an urge to remove from my head, from my chest, from me, to release words, even when I am not sure what those words are.

When I was little, I would feel this urge, and in my mind, I would picture myself climbing atop a classroom desk and screaming. Just to release the tightness in my head, my chest, from me; even though there were no words.

I can numb the tightness with mindless activities, but it will come back and it will be worse. So, I will try again, to release the tightness from my head, my chest, from me.

I don't think I was wrong as a child to feel that I needed to scream. I didn't scream but I really, really wanted to. Now I think it's just words. So, I write them, even when I don't know what to write.

Just to release the tightness from my head, my chest, from me.

IF THE ROCK RETWEETED YOUR POST

February 12, 2020

Basically. Life is life.

Sometimes it sucks. Sometimes it rocks.

Sometimes it's comme ci, comme ça.

If your minute is sucking right now, please know it's a minute. If your minute is amazing, celebrate the freaking hell out of it!!!

That's life – no matter how you look at it – like a wheel, as a graph, whatever, there are ups and downs.

You're supposed to cry.

You're supposed to laugh.

You're supposed to stub your toe and drop things.

You're supposed to burst with happiness and smell your baby's hair.

You're even allowed to do all those things at once.

No, I'm not advocating dropping babies, but if your baby slid off your lap this morning, kiss her and stop beating yourself up.

If you dropped your phone and cracked it because you were so excited that The Rock retweeted your post – it's ok! The freaking Rock retweeted your post! Of course, you dropped your damn phone!

That's life.

One minute at a time.

LIFE IS NOT A HIGHLIGHT REEL

March 7, 2020

On social media, we try to put our best foot forward. We zoom in on the tidy part of our kitchen, just slightly to the left of the dirty dishes in the sink. We are seen playing with our happy kids, walking in the sunshine, travelling, drinking perfectly foamed lattes, and laughing with our friends. We post perfectly made-up selfies with the exact amount of natural light shining across us in our beds and claim that we just woke up like this.

We all do this, to help us wipe away our insecurities about where we don't show up in our own lives as perfectly as we would like. We also know when we scroll through our feeds and see these pictures what goes on behind the scenes, and yet we still feel less than. Less than the mommy with the perfect baby bump, while ours are covered in stretch marks; less than the 5 beautiful women out for brunch at the most expensive restaurant in their fabulous city; less than the kids who are cheerfully riding horses at 2; less than the person who is travelling for business every single week. Because we only see the single picture, edited and changed, and magicked. We only read the short caption that says the new mommy cannot wait for baby Aromatherapy to arrive; that says "love these ladies! #babeswhobrunch"; that says Xander is such a horseman!! Just like his daddy! that says "jet setting! Another day, another plane!". We don't see a post about the absolute heart-wrenching breakdown that the mama-to-be had yesterday when she couldn't figure out how to build the baby stroller; the post about the bank balance after the brunch that makes it hard to pay her rent; the post about Xander screaming for 35 minutes about not wanting to be in the car to get to the riding stables; the post about the physical and emotional toll that all the travel has had on the business person and his family. We just don't, because our social media is our highlight reel. It is the stuff we want people to believe about us. We manipulate it to suit us because we want to be liked. We want to be the Joneses.

So, here is my real reel: I woke up like this, smudged makeup and all…

Sort of, the filters are not real.

There are 4 other selfies like this on my phone. The Portrait Mode on my phone creates unnatural natural light. Even though my make up is smudged, I "worked my angles". I am exhausted, my daughter is sick, I have cancelled my whole day to spend it in my pyjamas and drinking coffee. I am working on my budget, because I need to spend smarter. I am still in bed at 11am, because my muscles and joints are flaring. I sometimes feel jealous of other people and their success, and then tell myself that they are successful because they are not still laying in bed at 11am on a Saturday. I am not always as chill as I would like to be. Sometimes I fight with my husband. Sometimes my kids annoy me and sometimes I annoy them. Sometimes I read short books to catch up on my reading challenge quota for the year. Sometimes I feel like I will make a huge impact on the world and feel happy with my place in it. Sometimes I feel like I am worth nothing and cannot even dare to try to make an impact.

And sometimes I am just Kali.

Just me.

No highlight reels.

No filters.

Just me.

HAPPY INTERNATIONAL WOMEN'S DAY!

March 8, 2020

Happy International Women's Day!

If the last few years of chaos on this planet have brought anything of value to the world it is the new wave of feminism that is rolling through.

We are organizing and activating and empowering and advocating and marching and suing and standing up and shouting and writing and photographing and supporting and defending and believing and encouraging and dedicating and making and breaking and baring and singing and letting ourselves be seen. We are holding hands with our sisters and are mad as hell. We are recognizing that there is no one way to be a woman.

There is no ladylike. As women we are strong, and sweet, and fierce, and brave, and timid, and loud, and shy, and beautiful, and thin, and fat, and made up, and natural, and have acne, and flawless skin, and wear heels, and wellies, and paint our nails, and flip the bird, and wear diamonds, and have tattoos, and are mothers, and are childfree, and are sisters, and wives, and girlfriends, and daughters, and straight, and gay, and transgendered, and are models, and truckers, and teachers, and CEOs, and farmers. We are partners, and we are self-partnered, and we are proud, and we are smart, and we are everywhere and everyone.

To my fierce, beautiful, brave, funny, iconic, intelligent, artistic, creative, kind, clever and amazing ladies, I love you and respect you and will always be here for you. Today is for you.

THANK YOU. WE SEE YOU
~ COVID-19

March 14, 2020

Thank you to every single person working in health care right now. We see you, trying to calm fears, treat all sorts of patients, panicked people, in hot, uncomfortable masks and splash screens and covering gowns. We see you trying to keep people calm, and recommending medications, and checking fevers. Thank you so much.

Thank you to every single person working in retail trying to calm hysterical toilet paper hunters, trying to avoid bringing the virus and fear home to their kids. We see you being treated like personal gofers for every panicked shopper, trying to find every carton of cold and flu remedy, while being yelled at for not having face masks and hand sanitizer. Thank you so much.

Thank you to every single person who is showing kindness and patience. Thank you to every single person who is trying to remember not to touch their faces and is leaving the last packet of toilet paper on the shelf because they have some at home. Thank you to all the people who are taking proper precautions and practicing the phrase of the week "social distancing". Thank you so much.

We can do this. We just need to remember to be kind and grateful and patient. We need to remember to see each other.

DAY 1 – SPRING BREAK WITH COVID-19

March 17, 2020

"If you are abroad, it's time for you to come home." PM Justin Trudeau March 16, 2020

I went for a walk this morning with one of my best friends, and as we tramped in the early morning sun, I decided that I felt grateful that the weather was refusing to dim because my mood, our moods, and the general feeling in the air was sombre and on edge. It was a weird, beautiful feeling that God/the Universe/Mother Nature/The Goddess/Allah/whoever you believe in/the meteorologist(?) was lending us this beautiful day because they knew that we would need all the help we could get to keep from full-fledged pandemonium. COVID-19 is real. It's real, and we are social distancing and self-isolating, and doing all the things that can result in depression in a person, like me, who is prone to mental health struggles. The Universe cleared the air and pulled me out of doors to remember to play the Glad Game.

After our walk, my friend left to care for her piggies and to get the rest she would need to manage her workload. She works the graveyard shift at one of the local grocery stores and knew that today would be weird. The order would be huge, 5 times larger than a usual evening. The cleaning supplies and toilet paper, should they arrive at all, would be to replenish shelves that had never been so bare. People are scared.

I returned to my quiet home, kids and Dave still snug in their safe beds and began to work while I waited for the promised 10AM press conference, refilling my coffee twice while I waited for Trudeau to appear. I wanted reassurance. There would be none today.

The incongruity of the beautiful, brilliant blue sky against the knowledge that our borders were to be closed to all non-Canadians and permanent residents struck me. It reminded me of the last time that I was glued to the news with a similar feeling of dread – September 11, 2001. The brilliant blue sky, bright sunshine, and freshness of the air didn't fit with the anxiety and, as one of my best friends aptly called it, a sense of doom.

Prime Minister Justin Trudeau appeared 40 minutes late to address Canadians, and he was an embodiment of the anxiety that has gripped our world over the last few weeks, and particularly the last few days. When the leader of your nation is beautiful enough to appear on Rolling Stone, it is rare to see him looking tired and rumpled, hair out of place, eyes tired, skin pale. The moment he descended the steps of his home and took his place at the podium conveniently placed on his drive, it was clear that things were worse than I had expected, known, or hoped.

There will be no train rides into the city for a while. There will be no rides anywhere at all. Work will be done at home. Even if I could convince my crummy immune system to go out in public, what would I do? There is nowhere to go. As of today, offices are closing. Borders are closing. Bars and restaurants are closing. Casinos are closing. Museums. Airports. Theatres. Stores. Malls. Starbucks. Sporting events. Tim Horton's. Schools. Libraries. Gyms. My yoga studio. My meditation space. My volunteer commitments are on hold. BC Ferries is allowing people to remain in their vehicles on the car decks. Universities are releasing their students to study online without the infrastructure to handle that.

It's hard to reconcile this world and to parent responsibly in the uncertainty. It's hard to instil caution, without tipping into a panic. My kids are intuitive and can tell when things are weird or not right. How much do they need to know about the scariness? I don't want to be an alarmist, but I need them to be aware of the world around them. The rolling of the eyes and the mamaaaaaaaaas can get me to the point that I want to shout "are you crazy???? We are not going to the damn mall to get sick just to get Jell-O!" But somehow, I think that seeing their mother absolutely lose her mind would be more upsetting than anything they would see outside.

I will continue to watch the news; to plan for the worst and hope for the best. I will continue to feel grateful that people are so easily connected now, that we can strive to avoid falling victim to the loneliness that will pull us out of our self-isolation. We can still see what is happening in the world. We can still get food. We can still talk to our best friends and our family. We can still move forward and hopefully pull together – leaving a metre between us, in groups of no more than 50 – and save each other.

DAY 2 – ST PATRICK'S DAY DON'TS DURING COVID-19

March 19, 2020

It's St Patrick's Day. I'm usually all over making either an everything green or a traditional Irish dinner every year. No, we're not Irish, as far as I know, but I am all over a celebration that talks about luck and blessings. Plus, in my understanding, he chased all the snakes out of Ireland! (Allegory, you say. Meh! Don't ruin it for me!!)

March 17, 2020 was not typical for us. There were no shamrocks, no Shamrock Shakes, no Kiss Me I'm Irish napkins, no over the top feast of stew, soda bread, and the honorary can of Guinness (which never gets opened, and then is annually donated to my best friend's husband). None. There were chicken legs in the air fryer for the kids, smiley face McCain's mash potato/fries/thingies, and Brussels sprouts. There was my annual insistence that my green eyes absolutely DO count as wearing green, and there was anxiety. I certainly would have liked to do something for my kids, but between the overwhelming anxiety and fear, the lack of ability to enter the community, work, and everything else, it was not something that became prioritized. We did the math, we did read. I listened to a less than great audiobook by the daughter of BTK – if you are looking for harrowing hiking trails and Christian rebirth, then this may just be the book for you! I tried to convince my 12-year-old daughter filling Saran Wrap with beverages and popping them in her mouth was a choking hazard. This TikTok trend called jelly fruits (interesting since there is no fruit, nor jelly anywhere to be found) seems to promote the idea that if your parents didn't let you bite a balloon and choke on it as a baby, here is your second shot at having a thin piece of plastic lodged in your windpipe!!! YAY!! My daughter Made jelly fruit- jelly fruits.

I went for a dreary walk with my friends – the clouds did not part for us as they did on Monday. We saw gorgeous open areas and trees, but I just could not bring my brain around to find glad. I felt despondent and weary. I was just tired.

COVID-19 continued to fear its ugly head, with 3 more reported deaths and nearly 100 new cases. Bars were ordered to close indefinitely. Public schools were ordered to cease operation indefinitely. Restaurants would only be able to offer to take out. The social distancing was increased from 1 meter to 2 meters. Groups congregating would have to be less than 50 people, down from the initial mandate of 250 people. The borders to the US (the last open border) were closed for non-essential travel. A member of my extended family and someone extremely important to members of my family was quarantined in the UK. There is no way to know when or if this person will be allowed home soon.

And yet? And yet we still have reports of such craven selfishness that people are taking it upon themselves to "prove" that this thing isn't real. It's hyped up. It's no big deal. They wander amongst the population putting everyone, including the most vulnerable sections of the same at risk. They clear out grocery stores of needed items of food. They laugh when they selfishly purchase all the meat/toilet paper/sanitizer/Lysol they can find, if they could sell it at a premium. People loudly proclaim that this is all a hoax… days before they are rushed to hospital with nasty symptoms that would stand to reason as COVID19. There is a feeling that humanity is falling apart and that the irreconcilable differences of the last few years have come up when we need to care for each other more than ever. There is a feeling that things can and will get worse. There is a feeling that all the dystopian authors and filmmakers were more prescient about human nature than anyone else.

And yet? And yet, there is a store opening special early morning or evening times for the elderly or those with special needs. There are people sharing information. People are picking up needed supplies for their friends or neighbours. There is space in the deep freeze for your siblings to put their food. Yoga studios are live-streaming classes for yogis who cannot attend the now-shuttered fitness studios. People are going outside. My parents dropped bags of vegan meat and seafood and lactose-free milk at our door on a total, but most welcome surprise! For once conversations are about something major, with severe repercussions, rather than about the other moms at the school drop off. Our cars are parked. We are lowering our overall waste and greenhouse gas emissions. The planet is healing, and if we can follow these simple, but apparently terrible mandates and rules together, we may just be able to get through this without Thanos snapping away half of the world's population.

DAY 5 – MY HEART IS BREAKING A LITTLE BIT

March 21, 2020

Today was a hard day. Not that it was any worse than any other COVID-19 day, not really, but it felt harder. Every conversation felt fraught. Every decision had to be measured. Every choice felt wrong.

For two days I have felt a tightening in my chest, and not in the "I had better get tested" kind of way, but in the "holy shit, the whole world is stopping" kind of way. For 2 days, I doubled my Ativan and played loud music and went for walks and drank tea, and it sort of quelled it. But today? Today my inner beasts got the better of me and the tightening in my chest gave way to gut-wrenching, wracking sobs. Not once, not twice, but all. Day. Long.

When I am not sobbing, I am stressing and on the verge of tears. Trying not to think about crying. I am scared. I am afraid. I am frustrated. I am angry. I cannot keep up. Information changes day by day; hell, we're at the point where it changes minute by minute. What is allowable in the morning is forbidden by the afternoon. What we should do is suddenly something that we must do. The messages are mixed.

"Get outside! It's good for your mental and physical health!"

"Why are you outside? Flatten the curve, you selfish bitch!"

"Stay in contact with loved ones. But not that kind of contact!"

"Stay in your homes with your immediate families, but also stay away from your family members!! Self-quarantine within your self-quarantine!"

"Well, you don't need to be *that* extreme, come on now! Don't you think you are being a bit silly?"

If there is one thing that I need in my life, it's rules. I feel safe when someone tells me exactly what to do when to do it, and how. I am a people pleaser. I try to be everything to everyone. So, when the goalpost keeps wandering off, I feel so confused and unmoored. I think I am doing the right thing, only to turn around and find out the right thing was two left-hand turns ago, and now I am well into "wrong thing" territory.

I am grateful for texting. I am grateful for FaceTime. I am grateful for a flexible organization that's setting us up to work from home. I am grateful that Dave is past the worst of his cancer. I am grateful for my family and my bestest friends. I am grateful for #quarantwine delivered by ninja cars. I am grateful for my group of meme texts. I am grateful for my parents bringing us all the seafood. I am grateful for my doctor doing telephone appointments. I am grateful for a safe, warm home to keep my kids inside. I am grateful to live in a country where our people are cared for and the government is taking measures to protect us. I am grateful for so much. But today? Today, I'm still sad. I am grateful, but I am frustrated. I am grateful, but I am confused. I am grateful, but I am afraid.

Today was a hard day. Not really any harder, and probably not the hardest. Just hard. If you're having a hard day, remember, as the East High Wildcats, we're all in this together. It sucks. But at least we aren't alone.

DAY 6 – IT'S OKAY THAT YOU ARE NOT FINE

March 22, 2020

It's ok that you're not fine. No one expects you to be. No one expects anything right now, and that's okay, too. How can you expect something amorphous? You are probably in your home worrying about your family and friends. You are concerned that you coughed today. Is it dry weather? Allergies? Dust? COVID? While many of us wait in anxiety for daily updates, there are hundreds of people who have never been so busy in their lives. Health care providers, hospital workers, grocery store clerks, pharmacy technicians, public health nurses and doctors, government, researchers, medical scientists are all scrambling to keep us safe, fed, informed, cared for, and treated. They are doing their best to keep society functioning. They are working to find a treatment or a cure, or at very least keep it from spreading.

I can almost guarantee that no one is alright, and we are all doing what we can to maintain some sense of sanity. Today, I worked at my desk and tried not to panic about the cough that has been sitting in my throat all day. While I did, my daughter made a pie with my sister, who lives on the opposite end of the country over FaceTime; my brother and sister-in-law dropped off provisions on our porch without any face to face interaction; my dear friends dropped off a beautiful mug (it's my collection obsession after books) and toilet paper; my husband cleaned our home; my son played with LEGO and his cousin on Fortnite, and my parents staved off their loneliness by adopting 2 kittens.

That sounds okay, right? That sounds like we are all okay? You're right! It does sound okay! But it's also not okay – my sister-in-law is worried about her brother quarantined in the UK; my kids couldn't hug me or kiss me all day just in case my cough is the harbinger of doom; my friends are being run ragged over the inconsistent shipments and demands of the grocery store; my son self-soothes by cuddling in my lap which was not available to him; my work was slowed by the heavy demand on the WIFI in my area; my mom is so lonely without her family that the potential of not adopting her new fur babies was heartbreaking to her… I could go on and on, with both okay things and not okay things. But why would I do that? It's okay to not be okay. It's okay to feel scared and to feel worried. Just remember – while we are scared at home, feeling useless, we are doing our parts to help our fellow citizens who are feeling more pressure than they have ever felt before.

DAY 7ISH – THE TEACHER IS FED UP

March 24, 2020

Dear COVID-19 Quarantiners,

In Canada, some of you may or may not know, that our Prime Minister, Justin Trudeau, used to be a middle and high school teacher. So, as much as he is a politician, he is also a teacher. And today? Today, the teacher was FED UP! In his daily press conference, he reached a whole new level of being sick of us and wanting to put us all in detention.

"We've all seen the pictures online of people who seem to think they're invincible. Well, you're not. Enough is enough. Go home and stay home. This is what we all need to be doing," Mr. Trudeau informed his disruptive class of roughly 40 million children. His teacher's voice and stern face let us know that he was not messing around and that while yes, he may be the cool teacher who can plank with the best of them, he has his limit, and we have crossed it. He is done seeing us huddled in large groups, hosting weddings, and milling around like a carnival.

We all have reasons as to why we need to leave our homes occasionally. Some of us are not lucky enough to be able to stay inside. We are encouraged to go out for a run on our own, or get some fresh air, or go to work if we must, or bring groceries to our homebound neighbours. But for those of us who are acting like we are on a glorified vacation, wanting to get out and celebrate turning 19 with a pub crawl, Trudeau is fracking done with us. He warned us, and he warned us, and now we have pushed too far. So, to get back on the teacher's good side, and go back to the fun teacher who wears Star Wars socks on May the 4th, we had better do what he says, and stay home, if we have no reason to be out.

Remember – he said IF we have no reason to be out. This is not calling out people who are doing their best and staying, as a meme my sister-in-law sent me tonight, two beavers apart (get your head out of the gutter, Australia. The beaver is a fine and noble animal, just ask Joe Canuck). Call-out culture is not what Mr. Trudeau wants. He is in no mood for us to be lining up at his desk tattling on each other. He wants us to be kind, Canadian, and RESPECT THE RULES.

Sincerely,

Kali Desautels

Lifelong Teacher's Pet (32 years and holding)

DAY I-CAN'T-REMEMBER-WHICH – THE COVID SAGA CONTINUES

March 29, 2020

I like social media. A lot. I feel like it was created for introverts like me – just extroverted enough to want to say things that make people laugh, but overall, desperate for quiet space. I like to read what my friends are doing. I like to see pictures of their pets and kids. I like to mentally cheer for my family as they accomplish something. I like to direct the thoughts in my brain towards other people. I love to congratulate people on pregnancies, and engagements, and promotions, and weddings, and graduations. I like to click the little crying emoji on Facebook when someone is heartbroken, and I know that offering my thoughts and prayers will not be what is needed. I like taking videos of my kids, and then having them pop back up on my feed 3 or 4 years later, remember their big eyes, soft hair, and fat cheeks, frozen forever in time. I like being notified that someone I haven't seen since high school is having a birthday. I like everything about it, and in fact, am teased continuously for overusing it.

It's true. I do overuse social media. I check it multiple times a day, share too often, and like way too many pictures.

But I genuinely like to like them.

I have read articles about people's social media addictions, and the phantom cell phone alerts. I know that getting likes lights up the dopamine or oxytocin releasing section of my brain. But that also means that I know that it does that for other people as well. If I know that I can do something that will temporarily, but measurably cause an improvement in someone's day or mood, just by engaging with something that they posted online, why wouldn't I do this? Why shouldn't people know that their posting on Facebook through COVID-19 as the Star Trek Captain's log made me smile? (Thank you, Holly! It's awesome.)

Why shouldn't someone get 53 likes on a selfie of them with their engagement ring? They are excited and want to show it off. Why wouldn't I double click on someone's post about their ability to lift a truck? If it makes people happy, I like to do it. I like to make people feel happy.

Through the last few weeks, we have seen a lot of people reaching out to each other through social media. My friends and I have been doing online yoga and coffee dates. People are posting activities to do at home with their kids; posting pictures of their new COVID-19 foster/adopt pets. My sister is using the internet and social media to teach her son in Nova Scotia AND my kids in BC. My best friends and I have saved our sanity by sending each other memes that are either dark AF or inspiring depending on the mood. We are getting information, misinformation, and disinformation on Twitter. We are depending on social media for the social parts of our lives. Even the most introverted amongst us rely on people. We are social. It makes us feel good. We like each other. And so, right now, most of us are reaching for our devices and liking each other's posts.

And why not? If we can do something right now, that makes our friends and family feel good, when we are all on edge on day 50009090023 of quarantine… (ok, more like day 12…) why not?

FINDING THE QUIET MOMENTS

March 29, 2020

One of the things I love about my job is that it can be remote, and I can work from home regularly, so the switch to COVID-19 working from home didn't feel like a huge change.

The biggest challenge is that usually I have a very quiet house for 6 of the 8 hours while my kids are at school, and my recovering husband mostly sleeps. During COVID, the house is full, and there is very little quiet time, so I am working in all the available spaces, like when my son is busy yelling at his friends on Fortnite and my daughter is practicing elaborate makeup routines that I, as a 37-year-old woman, can't even imagine mastering.

This morning, with my cup of coffee, generously furnished by my family, my desktop on the kitchen table (back pain has me working my way back to my desk) and at least an hour of solitude, (minus shouts of "Look out for that sniper!! Why didn't you rumble? There's a Peely over there!!" And peals of laughter from my son's room) to get some of my work done. The best part about it? I literally love my job, so it doesn't feel like work. It feels like something that I look forward to and am lucky enough to do.

So happy Sunday. Try to find a way to make it happy, whatever your happy looks like.

20 THINGS I HAVE LEARNED IN QUARANTINE

April 5, 2020

Moving into the 4th week of a 2-week quarantine and I have a few things to say:

1) I still have all 4 members of my family, safe and sound (including Timon);

2) Texting my friends and family keeps me sane and smiling;

3) I have a fantastic job that I genuinely love that can be done from my home;

4) Society depends on us all working together because we are all dependent on each other;

5) Nationalist policies will never solve a global pandemic;

6) Dr. Bonnie Henry is the most calming person in the world, even when she is sharing bad news;

7) I love the 7pm honking and cheering, even though I live nowhere near a hospital, for the purpose of gratitude, and for the fortification of the community;

8) I don't really like leaving my house anyway, so staying in it 24/7 isn't that big of a deal;

9) Glennon Doyle's book Untamed is so good that it can be read in one day;

10) Things that stress me out, like baking, is soothing for other people;

11) My kids can want to kill each other one minute, and curl up and read together the next minute;

12) Chest tightness can be caused by anxiety AND be anxiety causing;

13) Skype is one of the greatest inventions in the world;

14) I stand by my belief that vaccines save lives and do not want to live in a world with less than 50% herd immunity;

15) Less pollution is taking the frizz from my hair;

16) We can heal the planet and ourselves by all working together;

17) This pandemic is being faced by everyone from janitors to billionaires, and cannot be faced by only one group or another;

18) We need each other, we need to support each other, we need to care about each other;

19) Small business owners are struggling, and need us to support them;

And finally, 20) there is no wrong way to handle this pandemic, other than to disregard the rules, orders, and scientists.

QUARANTINE MONTH 2:
REBOOTING

April 10, 2020

This week was hard. Not because I couldn't leave my house but because I had too many things happening in one week. My anxiety level reached an all-time high. I haven't felt that anxious in at least a year. Not since I was waiting for my husband's official cancer diagnosis. I was working on something super important for work, along with a few other personal things, including but not limited to – my son breaking quarantine, my husband being in more pain than he had been for a while, my daughter's school stress, my critical project at work… just all the things at once.

So, I started walking as fast as I could for 5km. I started walking in the grass barefoot. I started walking into the creek and letting the icy glacial water run over my feet. I started listening to Zen and the Art of Motorcycle Maintenance while staring up at the trees. I tried to breathe. I survived the week and turned in my project. It was Thursday before the long weekend, and I could feel my body burnout or my brain or my eyes or my soul. I don't know. Something. Something burned out. So, I ordered pizza and pasta for my family, and celebrated my survival of the week, because it truly felt like surviving, by going to bed at 5:35pm, waking slightly at the 7pm cheer, before returning to sleep.

I slept until 6:30am and moved into the living room to start my day, where I fell asleep until 9am, and then 10:30am, and then 12:15pm. This is surviving. The sleep of the burnout. The sleep of a hundred sleepless nights caught up with me. The sleep of anxiety. The sleep of self-protection and recovery. It's not productive. It's not catching up. It's rebooting.

And so today is « Good Friday », and I have slept most of it away. My daughter is sewing in her room, her machine sounding like an angry woodpecker on a streetlamp. My son is reading in his room. My husband is in the basement, either in his shop or on his game. My cat is at my feet and I am in bed. Again. Not resting, not sleeping, just here. Stream of consciousness blogging about nothing.

Rebooting.

"KINDNESS IS LOANING SOMEONE YOUR STRENGTH INSTEAD OF REMINDING THEM OF THEIR WEAKNESS." ~ ANDY STANLEY

April 21, 2020

"Kindness is loaning someone your strength instead of reminding them of their weakness." ~ Andy Stanley

We all suck. And we all rock.

We all have shame. And we all have pride.

We are all human.

It's so easy to try to make yourself feel better by pointing out how someone is failing worse than you are. For a moment you get that delicious moment of smugness…

…right before you walk into a door that says pull, instead of push.

As you get up and furtively look around to see if someone is looking, remember that we all fail at things.

All of us do.

It's just being human.

When you choose to find pleasure in someone else failing, you are choosing meanness and smallness, because kicking someone when they are already down doesn't make you the stronger, "better" person – it makes you a bully.

Yes – like it or not, even as adults we can be bullies.

Next time choose to be kind.

Choose to share your strength, because I guarantee that no matter how it seems on the outside, that person is struggling hard, and already knows the flaws that you so generously pointed out.

YOU'RE EVERYWHERE, ALL OF THE TIME.

April 21, 2020

Sometimes I just miss you.

Sometimes a memory will make me smile to think of you.

Sometimes I feel you with me or smell your old leather jacket, and a hint of WD-40, musk, and you.

I can't hear you in my head anymore. I really, really want to. I *know* what you sound like, but I can't hear it. There's a difference, trust me.

Sometimes I am ok. Sometimes I'm really, not.

When you left, I drove home screaming for you to come back. Even then I knew it wasn't possible, but I couldn't stop screaming for you. Dave drove behind me to make sure I got home safely.

I don't scream for you anymore. Not out loud anyway. I still cry for you though. Sometimes I can go months without being overcome by grief. Sometimes it comes in waves and breaks over me. It's easier on those days to just let it come. I know you wouldn't want me to cry, but I do. I know you would understand. You're not here anymore, and you're everywhere all the time.

You're Oreo cookies and coffee and lilac bushes and resting my eyes and parallel parking and blue-grey eyes and slapstick comedy and filming my kids and Blue Christmas and Mahalia Jackson.

You're airplanes and Hawaiian sunsets and scratched metal measuring tapes.

You're my hand cupping my chin when I'm thinking, and thick hair and silent belly laugh and hockey skates on ice.

You're spare change rattling in my pocket and the smell of Canadian Tire and taking a trip to the hardware store.

I liked to be your girl. I still like to be your girl. I am old enough to know that I will always miss you. I will never go a single day without thinking of you. I don't think April 21st will ever be anything but Grampa's birthday. I hope that you are sitting down and enjoying your cake.

I hope that you know that we are remembering you. All of you.

Fixing the dishwasher, having a hot water in the "zapper" for 90 seconds, teasing every child and animal you met, driving with both feet on an automatic, coming up with logical solutions, wearing your heavy black shoes, giving scratchy good night kisses.

I love you.

We all love you.

A LABOUR OF LOVE – POST-CANCER IS NOT POST-PAIN

April 22, 2020

You know what I would love? I would love to be able to tell you that since the cancer was removed, he is totally fine. I would love to give you an update on the magical life that he can live after his treatments. I would love to be able to tell you that he is thriving and getting along better than ever.

I could post this and say something about what a great husband he is to make dinner for us, and you would think "yeah, well, he wants to eat doesn't he? It's not your job to feed him!"

What you don't see is that this really is a labour of love. Sitting up, or standing, or lifting things, or even the simple act of eating is so strenuous on his body, it is like asking him to run a marathon and lift weights, rather than simply feeding his family. This is him, doing what he can, while he can, to show up for his family. After this, he quietly ate a small plate of the dinner, then went back to his space in the basement and was consumed by pain for the next 5 hours. Preparing the meal and eating it had taken so much out of him. What you don't see is the confusion at how he could be so consumed by pain months after he is meant to be healed.

What I hope you see is love. What I hope you see is that we are all struggling. What I hope you see is that therefore you are safe in your homes. What I hope you see is the reason that we cannot walk together and go for coffee. Because one day, I would love to give that update. One day I would love to tell you about the magical life he is leading after his recovery.

WHAT IS REALLY WORTH YOUR ENERGY?

April 24, 2020

What have I learned in the last year and a half?

I have learned to listen to my energy stores.

I have learned to focus on the things that give me energy.

I have learned to focus on the people and things that feel likewise energy outputs.

I have learned who I can talk to about what, and who I cannot.

I have learned that money is energy and where I spend my money reflects my values.

I have learned that a clean, uncluttered home restores my energy.

I have learned that I need fresh air and nature.

I have learned that there is a difference between self-improvement and changing oneself to fit in.

I have learned that if I can manage pigeon and frog pose, I can manage anything.

I have learned that taking advice is not mandatory and can be adapted to fit my needs.

I have learned that I know and love my family because of our differences, not despite them.

I learned that I have the right and the responsibility to respect myself.

I have learned that I can live with less, and in fact thrive with less.

I have learned that I stronger, bravery, and more patient than I thought I was.

I have learned that my kids' happiness is a direct reflection of my own.

I have learned that I still know how to put my hand up when I think I have the answer.

Most of all, I have learned that I must spend my energy wisely to survive both good and hard times; and that those two things are not mutually exclusive.

Things can be good AND can be hard.

MY DREAM HOME

April 29, 2020

Yesterday, I went for a walk. I was heading for my brother and sister-in-law's house and ended up nowhere near it. They live about 3.5km from me. I ended up in parts of my town that I had no idea even existed and was so lost I am not sure I could find my way back if I had directions.

It is important to note that getting lost is nothing new for me. I am so directionally challenged that my husband bought me a GPS for my car when TomToms were a thing. If you ask me for street names, I will maybe know 4 out of 8. But if you ask me how to get to most of them, it's unlikely to end well.

This doesn't bother me, however. It used to because I was convinced that some boogeyman was in the brush waiting to haul me off into the darkness (even at midday). But it's doesn't anymore. Mostly, while in my car, if I get lost, sooner or later the GPS on my phone will get me where I am going. There are only so many directions that a car can go.

But on foot? On foot getting lost is magical!! On foot I can go anywhere there isn't a no trespassing sign. On foot, I am vividly aware of my surroundings and notice moss on the tops of trees and sunlight through leaves. I can walk on the grass and feel the sponginess of the earth. I can feel the hard, smoothness of the pavement. I can feel the small pressure points of the gravel. (Including the ones that conveniently scrunch their way into the crevices of my sneaker soles).

When I got lost yesterday, I found my dream home. My picture book log cabin, in a knell, surrounded by a beautiful garden, old-growth trees, and cornering up to the creek. My dream home not 15 minutes away. On foot.

So now? Now I need to keep getting lost and finding the magical, wonderful, curious treasures. And I must wish for this house to be ready for me when I am ready for it.

Manufactured by Amazon.ca
Bolton, ON